Cutting Through
the Hype

REVISED | EXPANDED | UPDATED EDITION

Cutting Through the Hype

The Essential Guide to School Reform

Jane L. David and Larry Cuban

HARVARD EDUCATION PRESS

Cambridge, Massachusetts

Library of Congress Control Number 2010931320

Paperback ISBN 978-1-934742-70-9
Library Edition ISBN 978-1-934742-71-6

Published by Harvard Education Press,
an imprint of the Harvard Education Publishing Group

Harvard Education Press
8 Story Street
Cambridge, MA 02138

Cover Design: Sarah Henderson
Interior Design: Ralph L. Fowler

The typeface used in this book is Fairfield LH.

To my remarkable mother, Ruth,

and to my soul mate, David, for their

unwavering love and support.

—JLD

To Barbara (1937–2009),

for her enduring love, heartfelt wisdom,

and unshakeable strength.

—LC

Contents

PART THREE

Reforming Teaching and Learning

Preface

Our collaboration on this book comes out of a forty-five-year friendship that began in August 1966 at Cardozo High School in Washington, D.C.

In 1963 Larry left a high school teaching job in a Cleveland ghetto to become a master teacher in history for the Cardozo Project in Urban Teaching, a school-based university program training returned Peace Corps volunteers and recent college graduates to become teachers. In 1965 he became director of the program. In late August 1966, Larry was desperate. School was to start in less than two weeks, and he had just learned that the federal grant supporting the Cardozo Project would cover the hiring of two math interns. He had found one but had to have a second to justify a math program.

Jane, meanwhile, had just finished college in Oklahoma, one course shy of a math major. Heading east to find interesting work, she was about to give up after reading all the ads for secretaries and gal Fridays in New York and Boston. Having sworn off teaching and math, coming from a family of teachers, she was house-sitting for friends in Washington when the phone rang. A friend of the homeowners was calling everyone she knew trying to find an aspiring math teacher for her friend Larry Cuban.

Larry interviewed Jane the next day and, with some reluctance, due to her lack of enthusiasm about teaching, hired her on the spot. To the surprise of both, Jane loved teaching, in spite of the fact that it was by far the most difficult job she would ever hold. After several years, Jane left for graduate school at Harvard University to study education research and policy while Larry stayed on as a teacher in the District of Columbia and later moved to the central office to administer the district's staff development program.

After a brief stint in the federal government, Jane moved to Palo Alto, California, to work at a think tank and then on her own as an independent researcher and consultant, studying efforts to reform schools for poor and minority students. In 1981 Larry moved to Palo Alto to take a faculty position at Stanford University after serving as the superintendent of the Arlington (Virginia) Public Schools for seven years.

Since reuniting on the West Coast more than twenty-five years ago, we have met monthly for lunch or coffee. Many of the ideas in this book were topics of discussion and debate during those many lunches together. For both of us, teaching in an all-black inner-city school in the midst of the civil rights movement was a formative experience. Committed to the belief that public schools could be good schools for all students, we struggled with the ideals of the reform we were part of against the reality and tough challenges we faced daily: How to teach algebra to students who struggled with simple arithmetic. How to teach history to students who could barely read and had never left their neighborhood. How to get help for students in dire need of housing or medical attention. How to convince parents we were calling to report *good* news. Many of our assumptions were naive—we were innocent about the power of institutional patterns to shape behavior and the long-term effects of poverty and racism—just as many reformers' expectations today are naive.

To this day, we struggle with many of the same issues we had to face at Cardozo High School. We maintain a passionate commitment to the public school system—the backbone of an informed electorate and essential to a democratic society. We also maintain a fervent belief that reform is not only possible but also obligatory and that too many public schools in urban and rural America are shameful. In fact, it is this passion that leads us to raise questions about current reform policies, their implementation, and school practice. We also believe that our joint, rich experiences as teacher, administrator, researcher, evaluator, and historian have taught us a great deal about the promise and perils of school reform that will be valuable to district, state, and federal policymakers and to practitioners, parents, and concerned citizens—taxpayers all—who, like us, want to make schools better for all children.

Because a number of new reforms have appeared since we first wrote *Cutting Through the Hype*, we wanted to make it current. This second edition both updates and revises most of the chapters in the first edition and adds six new chapters capturing reforms of current interest. Since the introduction of No Child Left Behind in 2002 and initiatives from President Obama, the federal role and that of philanthropic foundations, evident in our first edition, have become far more pronounced in funding and in setting the policy agenda for reforming U.S. schools. New and revised chapters in this second edition reflect that shift in policy.

As in the first edition, here we have worked closely together in deciding which chapters needed updating, which had to be dropped, and which needed to be added. As before, we talked through each of these decisions, circulated drafts, and came to agreement amicably over our weekly lunch or coffee. Our collaboration for this second edition continues a tradition of discussing school reform that has lasted forty-five years. For this friendship and collegiality, we are most grateful.

Introduction

From Hype to Hope

E ACH YEAR, more and more well-intentioned reforms promise to make our schools better. From charters to small high schools, from high-stakes testing to teacher performance pay, from turnaround schools to laptops for every student—the waves of school reforms to make sense of keep coming, and their promises only grow. The momentum continues because Americans believe education is important, and what's important to the public is important to elected officials.

Political leaders capitalize on the public's concern about their schools, often overstating problems to mobilize support for their solutions while underestimating what teachers and principals have to do to make them work. Reform advocates and, increasingly, corporate and foundation leaders with the ear of policymakers shape school reforms based on some combination of ideology, best guesses, and hope. Seldom are those who must carry out the reforms—principals and teachers—involved in their design.

Meanwhile, researchers and educators have learned many important lessons from decades of ineffective reforms and their unintended side effects. Classroom teachers in particular have accumulated wisdom from trying to implement reforms designed by others. But those who propose reforms virtually never incorporate these important lessons into their mandates for improving schools.

The result is a growing chasm between policymakers' claims and the chance that the reforms will deliver what's promised. What's worse, even as their taxes underwrite new policies, voters in local, state, and national elections have no way to see beyond the hype. Nowhere can interested citizens—or even those who make policy—learn if a proposed reform has any chance of success or what it would take for that to happen. This book aims to fill that void.

Accumulated knowledge and wisdom are unlikely ever to be the driving forces behind enacted reforms. But these days politics too often plays a decisive role. A case in point: in 2004, New York City's mayor, elected by voters to take control of a failing school system, chose a Panel of Educational Inquiry and a new chancellor. The chancellor, in turn, proposed a policy that would force third graders to repeat the grade if they scored too low on the citywide reading and math tests. When a majority of the panel objected, the mayor intervened, fired his representatives on the panel, and appointed new members who voted for the chancellor's recommendation. In this case, naked political muscle trumped evidence.

Politics, however, can be tempered by information and understanding. Kindergartens, the comprehensive high school, vocational education, and Advanced Placement, for example, were all once proposed by broad-based political coalitions seeking school improvement. In each case, mixtures of ideologies, eye-catching slogans, occasional evidence, and fervent hopes carried the day.

In the past few decades, school reform has been the subject of more systematic study and documentation. Both researchers and practitioners paint similar pictures of the ebb and flow of reforms, what it takes to make them work, and why so many fail. Based on these sources and on our own decades of working in and studying individual schools and districts, we set out in this book to analyze many of the reforms that are prominent today. We spell out the assumptions underlying reforms that promise better teaching and learning, more effective schools, and more efficient school systems. We look at how well the reforms have worked and at what it would take for them to be more successful. Our goal is not to champion particular reforms but, instead, to offer balanced appraisals and reflect on hard-learned lessons.

Our intended audience encompasses many classes of citizens, including policymakers, from local school board members to those in state and federal offices; politicians and business leaders; advocates; educators; parents; union and foundation leaders; researchers in universities and think tanks; as well as other informed citizens. We collapse these many roles into three somewhat overlapping groups: policymakers, educators, and citizens. Policymakers include those who set policy and those who promote a particular reform. Educators include teachers and administrators, as well as those who work with and study them. Parents, individual advocates, and other concerned citizens are grouped together as citizens.

The more that policymakers, citizens, and educators understand what reforms can and cannot accomplish, the more they can make sense of the rhetoric that surrounds them. The more policymakers can separate rhetoric from reality and the more they understand about how schools really work, the more constructive their reform policies will be. The more that citizens and educators can make sense of reforms, the more they can participate in the political process that defines problems and propose workable policy solutions.

Just as media savvy is important in judging advertising hype, reform savvy is important in sorting out the kernel of truth in claims about reforms. And most reforms do have such a kernel. Getting computers into schools, for example, has become popular with policymakers over the past decade. The kernel of truth is that these technologies do in fact have great potential for teaching and learning. Yet putting information technology in classrooms and labs has not translated into frequent or imaginative use.

Many of the traps that reforms encounter are predictable. Others result from ignorance of the resources needed or unwillingness to invest enough to pull them off. No reform is a panacea, yet most of them are sold as if they are. In short, citizens, policymakers, and educators need to be wary of excessive promises, slick packaging, and flawed assumptions.

In this book, we scrutinize claims and jargon while attempting to get to the heart of three crucial questions: Does a reform make sense? Can the reform actually work in classrooms? Are the conditions for success in place? We chose to analyze reforms that have become part of the national discussion and are intended, directly or indirectly, to improve classroom teaching and student learning. For example, introducing performance-based pay for teachers or expanding the number of charter schools both ultimately aim to improve classroom practice.

The seeds of such reforms may have been planted by the White House, governors, state legislatures, mayors, foundations, unions, think tanks, corporate leaders, local school boards, or a range of others. All of the players try to extend their influence as ideas are reshaped into federal, state, or local policies. Some reform ideas are new. Many have appeared before, vanished, and were later resurrected. They are often pursued with a vengeance—witness the federal No Child Left Behind legislation with its reliance on tests and accountability—with varying degrees of understanding, support, or disdain from those who work in classrooms daily.

We offer the diagram entitled "The Many Influences on Reforms, from Policy to Practice" for those unfamiliar with the structure of America's decentralized tax-supported education system and the many influences that shape the reform-minded policies spilling forth from federal, state, and district offices. Oversimplified, of course, the diagram's purpose is to show the multilayered system of public schooling and the many players—elected and self-appointed— who introduce reform ideas that eventually become the policies that determine what schools must do. This policy-to-practice diagram also shows the variety of influences and the demands placed on elected officials to respond to school problems.

Policymakers at each level are the ones who have the authority and resources to take reform ideas and convert them into policies. Although policymakers have worthy aims for public education, they, like most of us, see the world from where they stand. They work in elected and appointed posts where they are constantly beset by individuals and groups seeking to influence their decisions. The arrows outside the box depict some of the many players representing varied interests (e.g., PTAs, unions, chambers of commerce, religious, ethnic and racial groups, CEOs) who lobby policymakers at all levels of the system, frequently and intensely. These interest groups seek either to initiate new or reshape existing school policies to benefit children—from their respective points of view.

The Many Influences on Reforms, from Policy to Practice

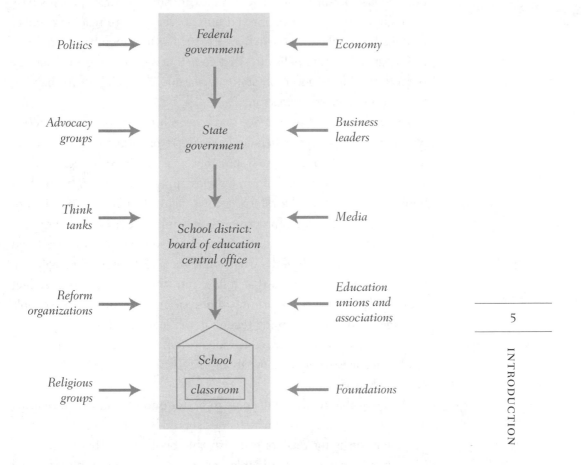

Federal, state, and local policymakers live in a world full of real and imagined crises often triggered by media accounts. Working in highly visible, conflict-ridden settings, policymakers typically listen to many voices and then latch onto what sounds like a good idea. They seldom have time to check out whether evidence supports their decision or whether, indeed, their idea will work when it is fleshed out and sent along to teachers. Almost none has ever taught, run a school, or super-intended a district. They are far removed from the classrooms where they expect their policies to make a difference.

Making the trip from policy to classroom practice is not easy. The journey is like the childhood game where you whisper something to one person who repeats the message to the next person and so on down the line. Typically, the initial message is vastly different from the one the last person hears. The same distortions occur as policies pass through layers of government and bureaucracy before reaching school principals and classroom teachers. One thing to remember in tracking the progression from policy to practice is that a reform message sent by the White House, governor, state legislature, or school board may not be the one received by teachers.

In our decades of experience and research in this policy-to-practice world, we have seen teachers and principals negotiate daily the twists and turns of school and classroom routines. We have participated in, watched, and researched reform policies aimed at improving what happens in classrooms. The reforms inevitably reflect the varied aims of policymakers seeking improvements in student learning by targeting changes in state systems of education, how schools are organized and governed, or, more directly, what is taught and how. Accordingly, we have grouped the reforms that follow into three sections that reflect these different levels: reforming the system, reforming how schools are organized, and reforming teaching and learning. Each chapter describes where a particular reform idea originated, the problem it is intended to solve, what we know about its effectiveness, and what it takes to make it work.

We hope that readers will come to better understand which reforms are worth investing in and which ones should be passed up. Ultimately, our intention is for readers to finish this book with a better grasp of what's realistic to expect of highly touted reforms, what trade-offs need to be considered, and what can be done to increase the likelihood that worthwhile reforms will succeed.

PART ONE

Reforming the System

In the United States, K–12 public education relies on a multilayered system in which states hold primary authority and responsibility for setting up and running their own public schools. Beyond that, the federal government contributes a small percentage of funding and a significant percentage of regulations. Finally, more than fifteen thousand local school districts make policy for over ninety thousand public schools within the constraints set by state and federal regulators.

The reforms we consider in this section include several launched by a number of states in the 1990s and incorporated into Title I of the federal No Child Left Behind Act of 2001 (NCLB): standards-based reform, test-based accountability, and efforts to close the achievement gap. We also look at charter schools, an example of parental choice, which generally traces its origins to state and local initiatives, although choice is a hallmark of NCLB. Rethinking teacher salaries (performance-based pay), shifting local power to the mayor (mayoral control), and expanding providers of teacher preparation (new pathways for teachers) are usually state or local initiatives.

1

Standards-Based Reform

"I HOPE THAT YOU will join me to define national goals in education for the first time. From this day forward let us be an America of tougher standards, of higher goals, and a land of bigger dreams."[1] These words, spoken by President George H. W. Bush during the national education summit in 1989, launched a national movement to set high academic standards for all students—a movement that has now survived three changes in administrations.

If students, like Olympic gymnasts, were judged against a set of challenging standards for performance instead of being compared with other students, schools would improve. Parents and employers would know what students had learned, not simply that they were better or worse than their peers. Moreover, if all students were held to the same high standards, struggling students would no longer face a watered-down curriculum, in effect denying them access to higher education and better jobs. It might take more time for some students, but all would be expected to succeed. These assumptions underlie standards-based reform. Easy to say, much harder to do.

No one can be against high standards; that would be tantamount to supporting low standards. Yet standards-based reform had barely begun before controversy erupted. Just beneath the surface were some sticky questions: What are the standards, and who chooses them? Are standards a sort of "Big Brother" measure telling everyone what to do or what goals to shoot for? What tests measure whether students meet standards? Where is the cutoff score for meeting standards, and who sets it? Should everyone be held to the same standards, even students with limited English proficiency and those with disabilities? And what happens to students—and their schools—who do not meet the standards?

Where Did the Idea Originate?

Spurred by reports in the mid-1980s of a failing public education system and a poor showing in international comparisons, state and national politicians and business leaders embraced the idea that schools, like businesses, should focus on results.[2] Moreover, these leaders believed that better performance on tests would be reflected in national economic productivity down the line. They were joined by advocates for poor and minority students, who felt such youngsters were being cheated by a watered-down curriculum and poor teaching. Strange bedfellows, they rallied around standards as a strategy for increasing international economic competitiveness and equity.

Like all grand policy ideas, reality trumped the rhetoric. In the early 1990s, the idea that education organizations or government-appointed committees could develop national standards fell prey to political spats and questions about the federal government's role. Criticism flew from all directions, agreeing only that the thousands of pages of standards produced by various groups were unworkable. Schools would have to run twenty-four hours a day to cover everything, the critics charged.

So the imagined ideal of a few really important big ideas in each subject for different grade levels bit the dust early. But this did not slow the momentum. By 1994, several states had designed standards-based systems, and major federal legislation incorporated the ideas of standards-based reform. Congress offered funds to get all states to develop standards-based systems and introduced the phrase "high standards" into the longstanding federal education program that provides aid to disadvantaged students, Title I of the Elementary and Secondary Education Act (ESEA). By 2002, the Title I legislation, rolled into an updated ESEA dubbed the No Child Left Behind Act, cast standards in terms of reaching "proficiency on challenging state academic achievement standards and state academic assessments."

And standards have never traveled alone. Since 2002, new policies from Washington and state capitals tied standards to testing and to accountability. Without tests matched to the new standards, no one would know whether students were learning everything they were supposed to learn. So, new tests would be needed to replace the old one-size-fits-all norm-referenced tests already used by schools nationwide.

Accountability became the watchword of the day. State and federal policymakers offered schools greater authority and flexibility to design their programs in exchange for accepting greater responsibility for student performance. Over time, the "authority and flexibility" side of the trade did not pan out for schools without sufficient resources and the help to figure out how to do a better job. Moreover, the "responsibility" side of the trade translated into more testing, with heavy penalties for failure to meet standards. In fact, federal and state policies began to decrease the flexibility of schools to design their own programs while increasing the accountability side of the bargain.

What Problem Is Standards-Based Reform Intended to Solve?

Standards-based reform tackles nothing less than overhauling the entire public school system. Its goal, in the words of corporate and political leaders, is to create a world-class education system, overcoming the perceived failure of the current system and thereby improving the nation's global economic competitiveness. To do so, in the words of IBM's former chairman and CEO Louis Gerstner Jr., "We either change it all—we commit to go all the way—or we fail. There's no in between."[3]

Beyond the rhetoric, a host of solutions are embedded in the idea of standards-based reform. Standards themselves represent a sea change in thinking about achievement. In a nation wedded to comparisons and percentile rankings, standards were intended to set a mark that all children must reach.

Standards were also expected to shift the emphasis from minimum competency or basic skills to higher-order skills. Although critics of public education pointed to a lackluster grasp of even the basics, high standards were expected to up the ante, leading not only to mastery of basic skills but also to proficiency in analysis, problem-solving, and communication skills deemed essential for twenty-first-century jobs. As a result, a school's test scores are now reported by percent of students proficient.

Standards-based reform also sought to shift the definition of fairness or equity from whether schools had similar resources to whether schools produced results (as measured by test scores) that showed improvement, not just overall but for groups that usually performed poorly. Schools now report test scores by subgroups. Test-based accountability for schools and students and penalties for failure to perform adequately were intended to motivate teachers and students to work harder to reach the high standards.

Does Standards-Based Reform Work?

Twenty years after the 1989 national education summit, President Barack Obama characterized the standards era up to 2010 as "a race to the bottom" and echoed President George H. W. Bush's push for tough standards: "I'm calling on our nation's governors and state education chiefs to develop standards and assessments that don't simply measure whether students can fill in a bubble on a test, but whether they possess twenty-first century skills like problem-solving and critical thinking and entrepreneurship and creativity."[4]

The hoped-for surge in student achievement did not materialize, even in states which lowered the bar for reaching their standards. Still, there's no doubt that standards-based reform has made a big impact. Every state has standards and tests that determine whether students are "proficient" as required by federal law. The language of standards has permeated the nation's schools; almost every classroom has state standards posted somewhere on the wall—sometimes simply referred to by number. Equally prominent is the change in how results are reported. To some this represents progress: a focus on results and attention to often-ignored subgroups, such as African American and Hispanic students. To others these same shifts represent backsliding: an overemphasis on annual standardized tests and test preparation at the expense of teaching students how to think and apply what they know. Ample research supports both viewpoints—and many agree with both.

Have test scores gone up? Current data from the state and national level provide a mixed picture. National Assessment in Educational Progress (NAEP) long-term trend data do not show a pattern of increased scores from 1999 to 2008, when all states implemented NCLB, compared to the prior decade (1990–1999). Reading and math score increases were higher for nine-year-olds but not for thirteen- and seventeen-year-olds. For some states, in some subjects scores have increased. According to one analysis of state test scores, gaps between subgroups have narrowed somewhat but remain large.[5] NAEP state-by-state data from 2003 to 2007 show a consistent pattern of no change in gaps between whites and blacks or between whites and Latinos.[6]

When the measures shift from NAEP to state tests, it can be hard to make sense of test results because most states report scores in terms of percent of students reaching proficiency—a direct result of standards-based reform. But what this means differs from one state to the next and often from one year to the next in the same state.

For example, in 2000 North Carolina reported that 84 percent of fourth graders reached proficiency, which seems terrific, while Louisiana reported only 12 percent, a poor showing. However, on the National Assessment of Educational Progress, North Carolina looked less stellar: only 28 percent of North Carolina's students reached proficiency. In Louisiana, 14 percent reached proficiency on the national test—close to the results on their state tests. This suggests that Louisiana had much tougher standards for performance.[7]

Given the demands of NCLB to bring all students to the proficient level by 2014, states with high standards have a much longer and harder road than those with low standards. Not surprisingly, several states have already lowered their standards. For example, in 2004 Arizona rewrote the state test and lowered the passing scores for every grade and subject. To boost scores further, they provided guides to teachers on what the test would cover and made sample tests available online.

Passing rates increased as much as 30 percentage points.[8] As 2014 approaches, other states are following this path. Between 2005 and 2007, sixteen states lowered their standards for reaching proficiency on eighth-grade mathematics exams.[9] Without such actions, states would face the equivalent of a balloon payment on a mortgage. Because these adjustments are political, not educational, decisions, they have fueled the current press for more rigorous standards across all states. In 2009, the National Governors' Association and the Council of Chief State School Officers began an effort to develop a more streamlined and rigorous set of standards in English language arts and mathematics.

What is the likelihood that more rigorous standards will change the outcomes from less rigorous standards? In 1989, the National Education Goals announced by the first President Bush were to be achieved by 2000. They were not. In 2002, NCLB required all states to have all students proficient by 2014. In 2010, that goal is clearly unattainable. The current administration has just floated the goal that all students will be ready for college or a career by 2020. Clearly, such statements are wishful thinking, designed for their symbolic value and their public relations appeal.

Ultimate judgments about the impact of standards-based reform will continue to be subject to debate because the original policy ideas have never been practiced. Instead of broad agreement on a few ambitious standards, most states have lengthy lists that enumerate every skill, reinforcing the frequent criticism that the American curriculum is a mile wide and an inch deep. Instead of new tests that show what students know and can do, most states use the same old ones. Instead of trading flexibility for accountability, schools actually have less discretion, more testing, and stiffer penalties for low test scores than they once did. In fact, under No Child Left Behind, these schools can improve substantially and still be penalized. Finally, the idea that schools would have the resources and training needed to teach to high standards never completely gained traction among state and federal policymakers.

One can imagine a new set of common core standards with federal monetary incentives for states to adopt them, but the likelihood seems slim that the fundamental barriers to improvement would change—especially tests that get at real learning and the know-how for teachers and leaders to do a better job.

So the good news is that high standards for all students coupled with reporting results by subgroups, such as student ethnicity and poverty, have focused attention on raising those at the bottom. It keeps the public and educators aware that tremendous effort and resources are needed to accelerate the learning of the lowest-scoring students, those who have the longest way to go. Standards-based reform has also zeroed in on test performance, leading in some cases to more careful tracking of the progress of individual students and to better attempts to help them.

The Solution, in Our View

In theory, standards-based reform offers a strong starting point for strengthening public education. With broad support and a realistic scope, standards can set high expectations for what students should know and be able to do. With well-designed assessments and attainable goals, schools and districts can carefully track whether particular groups of students are lagging behind. So the solution is not to abandon standards or ignore the students most likely to perform poorly. Instead, the solution lies in figuring out what it takes for schools to meet high standards, especially those with the highest concentrations of minority and poor children, which typically have the fewest well-trained and well-seasoned teachers.[10] Simply testing these students more—and narrowing the curriculum to prepare them for tests—is not the answer. The bold vision behind standards begs for serious attention to good teaching, strong curriculum materials, tests that truly capture what we want students to learn, and help for students who need it.

2

Test-Based Accountability

ACROSS THE COUNTRY, teachers prepare students for the state tests they will take each spring. The stakes are high. Federal legislation has made standardized tests the basis for determining whether students and schools have met the proficiency targets set by their states. Failure to meet the targets can have serious consequences in some cases, whether a student graduates, a school is restaffed or closed, or the state takes over a district.

The rhetoric of accountability appeals to legislators and to the public: high stakes will put pressure on students and teachers to improve, scores will go up, and, as written in NCLB, all students will reach proficiency by 2014. The argument begs the question of how top-down pressure to improve translates into better classroom teaching and more learning. Do scores go up? And if they do, does that signify more learning? Or have teachers and students simply learned how to "play the game"—figuring out what is likely to be on the test and concentrating on those topics?

Where Did High-Stakes Testing Originate?

Standardized tests have been a staple of American public education for nearly a century. Together with teacher recommendations, test scores have been used to place students in particular programs or tracks. What is significantly different today is that nearly all states and the federal government rely on test scores alone to make high-stakes judgments about students and teachers, and penalties follow if performance does not meet targets.

This major shift in emphasis stems from the same source that launched standards-based reform: a coalition of business leaders, politicians, and policy advisers who argued that the nation's performance on international tests is tied to economic productivity. Policymakers saw the United States' low ranking on international tests relative to other countries and identified the public schools as the source of the problem. As other policymakers had done in the late nineteenth century, late-twentieth-century decision makers looked to business models for reform ideas. From that view, students' test scores became products, their parents customers, and taxpayers shareholders to whom the schools are accountable for results based on annual increases in test scores rather than profits.

In the 1990s, several states launched their own versions of high-stakes testing and accountability. Then, in 2002, the No Child Left Behind Act required all states to use nationally standardized tests and to set proficiency targets for most grade levels—called Adequate Yearly Progress (AYP)—and for subgroups of students (e.g., racial/ethnic groups and students with disabilities). States and districts are expected to help schools that fail to meet their targets and to provide alternative choices or extra services for students if their parents request them. Schools that continue to fail face more serious sanctions, including closure. Failing state tests required for high school graduation has equally serious consequences for individual students.

What Problem Is High-Stakes
Testing Intended to Solve?

"Accountability tests allow parents to know whether or not their children are truly learning. They are the key to unmasking problems in a system that for too long has allowed too many children to pass through without learning the basics needed to succeed."[1] This statement by Congressman John Boehner (R-OH) captures the broad sweep of problems that high-stakes testing is expected to solve. Parents want information about how their children are doing and how they stack up against others, while national and state policymakers seek big-picture accountability. However, test scores that point to weak spots in the public school system—which policymakers want to know about—do not tell individual parents anything about what or how much their child is learning. Nor do they give teachers the kind of information they need to improve their instruction for individual students.

The use of tests for high-stakes accountability to improve achievement rests on several critical assumptions. It assumes that tests measure what parents and teachers expect students to learn, what the public agrees on as the definition of proficient (or, how good is good enough?), and what the schools teach, not the student's background.

It's actually quite difficult to meet these assumptions, it turns out. No single test can measure everything. Standardized tests measure what policymakers and test designers think is important, and only a small fraction of that. Tests are given in some subjects but not others. They cover topics familiar to everyone (e.g., grammar, spelling, comprehension), but the items are chosen for technical reasons. For example, no item is included that everyone is likely to get right, and much of what is learned in school is not tested. Even when publishers declare their tests to be "aligned" to state standards, they can only address a handful of the dozens and dozens of standards and objectives. And they tend to choose those that are easy to measure, not those that capture big ideas and thinking skills.

When penalties are attached to test results, according to researchers, the tests become the curriculum. In fact, what is not on the test gets ignored. So entire subjects are not tested and therefore get short shrift—as do subjects that are tested, namely English and math, since items focus on what is easy to measure.

For all these reasons, testing experts like University of California, Los Angeles emeritus professor James Popham, Harvard University professor Daniel Koretz, and University of Colorado professor Robert Linn argue that standardized tests should not be used to judge school or teacher quality. They were originally created to show how students stack up against each other, not how much they have learned in school. Even when such tests claim to be "standards-based," the types of questions and criteria for inclusion are similar. Measuring school quality with a standardized test is "like measuring temperature with a tablespoon," according to Popham—a purpose for which it was not intended and for which it does a dreadful job.[2]

Because NCLB requires each state to define what it means to be proficient, the second assumption—that the public agrees on how good is good enough—has been put to the test. Each state picks a cutoff point for defining proficiency. In the fall of 2003, the percent of schools that failed to meet AYP ranged from 8 percent in Minnesota to 87 percent in Florida.[3] In 2008, analyses showed once again that whether a school makes AYP depends as much on the state in which it is located as on its students' performance.[4] This does not mean that some states have very high proportions of proficient students and others do not. It means that their definitions of proficiency differ.

Most states do not pick cutoff points based on consensus about what it means to be proficient. Choices are made by state-level committees based on their best guesses of how many students will fail. When they misjudge, the cutoff score changes. In Pennsylvania, for example, the state lowered the threshold for schools in 2004. Without the change, more than twice as many schools would have failed to meet the target.[5] In some states, cutoff scores determine whether a student can graduate from high school. Here, too, states retreat when faced with high rates of failure. For example, after high failure rates on New York State's new rigorous math exam in 2003, the results were set aside and the score for passing lowered.

The final assumption underlying high-stakes testing is that schools control what the tests measure. This is the most flawed assumption of all. The goal of high-stakes testing, as embodied in NCLB, is to ensure that all students reach proficiency. Yet students start school at very different places; some can already read, while others do not know the alphabet. Some can count to one hundred; others cannot count to ten. Moreover, students from families living in poverty, which are disproportionately minority families, are far more likely to be among those who start school behind their peers and often fall further and further behind.

The goal of NCLB is to pressure schools to make sure these students reach proficiency instead of falling behind. But this creates several challenges for schools: on the good side, reporting test scores by groups defined by race, poverty, language, and disability ensures that these students are not overlooked; but, at the same time, these students are the most likely to have low scores, bringing down scores for their schools as well. So schools with higher proportions of such students are less likely to meet their targets, even those with excellent teaching. Moreover, the more diverse the student population, the harder it is to meet the standard because it must be met by so many different subgroups.

To set the same high expectations for all students, the law prescribes measuring students each year against a fixed standard (e.g., percent scoring above the fiftieth percentile). Yet this approach masks strong gains in scores made by students who start very low but still do not reach the standard, frustrating both students and teachers.[6]

Allowing no excuses for poor-performing students sends an important message to educators; many teachers have for too long harbored low expectations for some students and simply given up on them. Yet, high expectations are not enough when teachers lack skills, students are unwilling, and parents cannot lend support.

These problems with the assumptions policymakers hold are not easily resolved. They point to the enormous responsibility placed on the public school system and the challenges schools face in meeting the high expectations of the nation. The question is whether the trade-offs embodied in high-stakes accountability do more good than harm or vice versa.

Does High-Stakes Testing Work?

Does external pressure on students and teachers to improve translate into better teaching and more learning? The simple answer is yes—and no. If the question is whether educators are paying more attention to all subgroups of students, the answer is yes. If the question is whether the scores go up, the answer is often yes. If the question is whether teaching and learning have actually improved, the answer is usually no.

Scores on high-stakes state tests have been increasing over the last decade in some states at some grade levels in some subjects. Whether these increases reflect more learning is far less certain.[7] Teachers and students become more familiar with the test and how to prepare for it. And they devote far more time to subjects and topics on the test.

The recent history of NCLB confirms this. Entire subjects have been dropped or relegated into short time slots, from science and social studies to music and art.[8] Although specific test items change from year to year, over a number of years, it is clear to educators which standards are emphasized and which not. So the tested topics are emphasized, which often means less attention to intellectual and social goals highly valued by parents and educators and future employers.

When state tests require writing and explanations of problem solving, test prep can be of a higher caliber than preparation for multiple-choice, fact-based questions. Some states tried to move in this direction, but most, such as Maryland, reversed course given the high costs of scoring items that are not multiple choice. Even when the tests are better, the teaching may not be because teachers are less well prepared. In the 1990s, studies of states with new kinds of tests, such as Kentucky and Maryland, found teachers trying to teach to more complicated tests designed to get at students' understanding of concepts, but the teachers themselves didn't know enough to do a good job of explaining the ideas.[9]

Comparisons to other tests help researchers determine whether higher scores on high-stakes tests reflect more learning. NAEP provides a national picture of progress across the years. Although the NAEP data for 2007 and 2008 show increases in scores for some ages in reading and math, the pattern of increases since 1971 does not match NCLB implementation.[10]

High-stakes accountability is "good for bad teachers and bad for good teachers," according to a mentor-teacher in an Arizona elementary school.[11] For teachers who have been doing little teaching, high-stakes testing can prod them into action. They will not turn into good teachers without considerable training and help, but they will teach. But for those who have been working hard at the job, the pressure can turn into anxiety and frustration over the limits of test preparation, not being able to teach other things, and simply not knowing what else to do to raise test scores.

Moreover, anxiety about high-stakes tests leads to troublesome results: in the worst-case scenarios, teachers and students cheat, students give up and drop out, or teachers leave poor schools for those with higher-performing students. For example, in 2004 the *Dallas Morning News* conducted an analysis of scores on the Texas Assessment of Knowledge and Skills (TAKS) and found "strong evidence of organized, teacher-led cheating on the TAKS test in dozens of Texas schools and suspicious scores in hundreds more."[12] A Cato Institute report claims that NCLB "obviously increases the incentives for cheating" and anticipates more in the future, "both detected and undetected."[13]

TESTING AT ITS BEST AND WORST

	The Good	The Bad	The Ugly
Teachers	What is on the test can lead teachers to teach things they have ignored and to teach kids they have ignored.	Nothing is taught except what is on the test. The curriculum becomes test prep.	Pressure to increase scores leads to cheating, and teachers ignore struggling students whose scores are unlikely to rise.
Students	Some students try harder when tests are tied to course grade or promotion.	Students don't learn important skills and knowledge.	Students give up and drop out.
Schools	Principals and teachers work together to figure out how to raise test scores.	Teachers don't know what to do so they resort to test prep and attending to the kids just below proficiency.	Principals and teachers leave low-performing (poor) schools to go to higher-performing (wealthier) schools.
Districts	District leaders pay attention to all the schools and help them improve.	District leaders don't know how to help schools improve.	The state takes over failing schools but doesn't know how to help them improve.

The real test of high-stakes testing is to be found in the remedies applied when schools or students fail. Do the consequences attached to poor performance actually improve teaching and learning? Standardized test scores do not provide teachers with any guidance on what they should do differently. States and districts are expected to help, but most lack enough people with the expertise to do the job. New programs and different textbooks may solve part of the problem, but a long history of research proves that programs are only as good as the people who put them into practice. Many great-sounding solutions—even those proven effective in other settings—founder when tried in new situations.

If districts fail to help schools, states are expected to take over. Yet states have no proven track record at being able to do this successfully; numerous examples exist of state failures to turn around districts. Even closing low-performing schools and reopening them with new staff has not proved successful. In California and Maryland such actions did not lead to improvement; in fact, some schools were worse off.[14] The same reasons that caused low performance in the first place did not disappear with a different set of hands on the helm.

The Solution, in Our View

Testing is not going away, but both the tests and the ways they are used can be greatly improved.

Proponents of standards-based reform emphasize the importance of good tests—tests that are closely tied to a reasonable set of standards and that both improve and go beyond multiple-choice items. Such tests are typically not those sold by national testing companies. One direction for improvement would be to break the stranglehold of a handful of national test publishers and invest in the development of better tests—tests that probe whether a student can ask good questions, set up an experiment, debate an issue, create a product, stick with a difficult task, and work with others. A second improvement would be to always base decisions with consequences on more than one measure.

Tests also should be used for the purposes for which they were designed. Policymakers need to monitor school progress, but they do not need information on every student in every subject. Like political polls and customer surveys, testing samples of students can monitor progress at lower cost and without the negative effects of high-stakes testing on individuals. No matter how good or how appropriate the test, however, decisions about the future of a student or a school should be based on more than one test score. Test scores are not perfectly accurate. Like poll results, they have margins of error and should be reported the same way. Because tests are imperfect, a student should not be denied a diploma on the basis of one exam. Nor should a single score determine a teacher's or a school's success or failure.

Better tests used more appropriately is a start, but only that. At the end of the day, the question is whether schools can get what they need to improve. External pressure may be an effective motivator for some, but it does not help principals and teachers know what they should do to raise student achievement.

3

Closing the
Achievement Gap

PICTURE A FIFTH-GRADE classroom in San Diego. The thirty-three students range from six newcomers who arrived from Mexico midyear and speak no English, to Hmong students who speak a little English, to white and Latino students who are fluent in English and high performing. The teacher struggles to provide challenging materials to his top students and to accelerate the learning of those at the bottom, hoping to close the achievement gap inside his classroom.

Imagine two schools in Chicago, one with all African American students from poor South Side families and the other with mostly affluent white students on the North Side. The principal of the South Side school knows his test scores will be much lower than the North Side school and wonders how he can increase test scores enough to begin to close the gap. Most of his entering kindergartners are unable to hold a pencil or recognize letters of the alphabet, while five-year-olds at the North Side school can already recognize many words and some can read.

Whether comparing students in a classroom or comparing schools in a district or comparing one district to another, achievement gaps among racial and economic groups persist. The intent behind closing these gaps is to break the connection between race or family income and achievement while at the same time continuing to improve the performance of the top students. For this to happen, the achievement of the lowest-performing students must increase at a much higher rate than those at the top. As in a race, those at the back of the pack have to run much faster than those in the lead to catch up.

Gaps between test score averages for black students and Hispanic students at the low end and white students at the high end have persisted for decades. The same gaps lie between the poorest students and their more affluent peers. The gaps are also evident in the rates for dropping out, taking college-prep courses, graduating from high school, and obtaining college degrees, and ultimately in the jobs the students get.

Real estate agents and scholars know that test scores reflect the wealth of a school's neighborhood. Well-to-do neighborhoods have schools with high test scores. In the United States, black and Hispanic families are more likely to be poor than white families, and therefore their children are more likely to post lower test scores. In fact, more than one-third of all African American children (43 percent) live in poverty, as do 30 percent of Hispanic children, compared with 10 percent of white children.[1]

To make matters worse, schools with mostly minority and poor students have fewer experienced teachers and fewer supplies than those with more affluent white students.[2] The same problem exists within schools: those performing least well are the most likely to get inexperienced teachers and low-level instruction. As one advocate put it, "We take kids who have less to begin with, and then we give them less in school, too."[3]

It is no surprise that test scores are more likely to be at the low end for both minority students and those from the least-wealthy families. The challenge is what to do about it.

Where Did the Idea of Closing the Achievement Gap Originate?

Achievement gaps between minority and white students and between poor and more affluent students have been documented for as long as the tools to measure them have existed. From 1970 to 2008, the gaps narrowed somewhat for some age groups, but the point spread remains large. For example, in spite of thirty-seven years of slowly increasing reading scores, black children have lower scores in 2008 than white children had in 1971.[4] The story is the same for Hispanic students.

The achievement gap reflects disparities in children's backgrounds on starting school—disparities that are then compounded by the gaps in funding, teacher expertise, and curriculum rigor that children encounter in school. Those who start the farthest behind usually attend schools with the fewest resources or are relegated to tracks within schools that offer the weakest academic program. As a result, the gap between poor children and their better-off peers widens as students move through school.

What is distinctly different today is the attention to achievement gaps and the dual beliefs among policymakers that all children can reach proficiency and that, with enough effort, schools alone can close the gaps. In response, "closing the gap" has become a mantra in schools and districts across the country.

This renewed attention results from state and federal requirements to report test results by racial groups and the specific requirement in NCLB that each group must show progress. The design of NCLB is modeled after Texas reforms launched in the 1980s, at the prodding of businessman H. Ross Perot, that required annual testing and reporting results by racial groups. In the 1990s, Governor George W. Bush introduced a new Texas test and by the end of the decade proclaimed that scores had climbed and achievement gaps were closing.[5]

But achievement gaps are averages, and averages can be dangerous. As statisticians are fond of saying, you can drown walking across a creek with an average depth of one foot. Many white students score lower than many black students. Many Hispanic students score higher than many white students. One danger in reporting data by racial group is the potential to reinforce stereotypes, encouraging educators to judge students based on race rather than on individual learning needs.

What Problem Is Closing the Achievement Gap Intended to Solve?

Closing the achievement gap represents the promise of America: providing equitable opportunities for all Americans to reach their full potential. Outside the family, the public schools serve as the primary venue for getting a shot at a college degree and a high-paying job. That some youngsters would do better than others has always been taken for granted. The dream is that those differences are not tied to particular racial or social-class groups.

Under standards-based reform, the goal of equitable opportunity has been restated. The aim is to ensure that all students reach a certain level of proficiency, based on each state's definition of proficiency. The challenge school systems face is how to close the gap without limiting what top students learn and without setting the bar so low that everyone can pass it.

Does Focusing Attention on Closing the Achievement Gap Work?

Federal and state requirements to report achievement test scores by racial groups—and to require progress for each—has been remarkably successful in drawing attention to achievement gaps. Educators and education policymakers all talk about the achievement gap—language that was noticeably absent in recent years. Even the acronym CTAG (closing the achievement gap) has been incorporated into the vocabulary of educators. The problem cannot be swept under the rug. Achievement gaps exist and need attention.

Whether paying more attention to achievement gaps results in narrowing them is not so clear. NAEP data indicate virtually no change in achievement gaps between minority groups and whites from 2003 to 2007, suggesting that No Child Left Behind has not succeeded in its goal to change this picture.[6] Black and Hispanic students scored much higher than they did thirty years ago, but most of those gains were made during desegregation in the 1970s and 1980s.[7] What's more, how gaps are calculated can result in different conclusions.[8]

Even where positive evidence is touted, it is rarely sustained and confirmed by other data sources. For example, an elementary school might demonstrate a smaller gap between white and Hispanic students this year compared with last year, but only in second-grade reading or fourth-grade math. Moreover, the following year the gap may not continue to decrease. Still, attention to gaps is a first step, and any progress deserves celebration.

Repeated studies show that it is possible for some schools to narrow achievement gaps. Studies that identify schools that beat the odds— those with mostly minority and poor students—inspire hope by demonstrating what is possible. But the number of schools that have done so consistently, over several years at most grade levels, is quite small and virtually nonexistent beyond elementary school. Moreover, what is learned from these schools runs up against the perennial problem of other school reforms: how to take ideas that work in one place and successfully transplant them in others.

Gaps also narrow or widen for reasons that have nothing to do with real improvements. Lowering a cut-off score can make it look as if gaps are narrowing, but it is merely a mirage, since those students at the bottom are not really learning more. Yet states are under enormous pressure to get more students to proficiency each year. Abigail Thernstrom, a member of the Massachusetts board of education, predicted that it would be impossible for all students to reach the state's proficiency level, which is roughly comparable to the definition of proficient under NAEP. "It's a ludicrous goal," she said. "We will have to define proficiency way down—I mean way, way down."[9]

The Solution, in Our View

Under NCLB, schools are expected not only to keep achievement gaps from widening but also to make up for whatever gaps exist when children enter school. This is a tall order.

It is not hard to see that the lowest-performing students cannot catch up unless they have much more time to learn and better instruction. More time means more instruction, after school or during the summer or during the school day, if it can be done without sacrificing other important learning goals. Better instruction means better teachers, more efficient use of time, and solid lessons. This means getting the best teachers and materials to the students who need them the most.

Getting the best to poor and minority students, especially when budgets are tight, can end up pitting wealthier, politically connected parents who also want the best for their children against poor parents with less political muscle. Does the public will exist to move the best teachers to the schools in the poorest neighborhoods and create conditions that allow them flourish? "The solution seems obvious," said Texas district judge John Dietz in his 2004 ruling on school funding in Texas. "Texas needs to close the education gap. But the rub is that it costs money to close the educational achievement gap."[10]

Moreover, many question whether schools alone can bridge the achievement gap, even with additional resources. It is one thing to have high hopes for all students. It is another to know how to dramatically speed up learning so struggling students catch up to their peers. Schools certainly have a role to play, but most scholars and policy analysts agree that efforts to close the gap must begin much earlier than kindergarten and outside the school. Without tackling the barriers to learning outside of school, educators' efforts can only go so far.

In its proclamations on closing the achievement gap, the National Governors' Association (NGA) emphasizes the importance of the first five years of a child's life, arguing that the need for young children to have stable, nurturing relationships, access to health care and proper nutrition, and early exposure to learning activities is paramount. Specifically, NGA recommends high-quality childcare, professional development for caregivers, preschool programs, health care and social services, and parent education, among others.[11]

Closing the gap cannot happen quickly, easily, or cheaply. It requires a balancing act: providing funds and keeping pressure on schools to expect the most from the students least well-off without setting unrealistic expectations and punishing schools for failing to meet them.

4

Charter Schools—
Parental Choice
at Work

"AN ESCAPE HATCH from broken systems." So goes the rhetoric of those promoting charters. And they have found a sympathetic ear among many urban parents and reformers who fear that large city districts are beyond repair and that poor minority students are being left behind.

Arguing that the public schools should operate like a marketplace, proponents of charters claim that expanded choices will spur urban schools to improve, as they compete for students who can choose among publicly funded alternatives rather than go to private schools. Parental choice has a long history, but only recently have the options become decidedly market-based and officially sanctioned in federal and state laws. At the same time, sharp and nasty conflict has dominated debates over using charters as a tool to revamp low-performing schools.

Giving options to parents who feel their children are trapped in lousy neighborhood schools has broad support, but doing so creates a new set of concerns. Parents in Dayton, Ohio, can choose from nearly thirty charter schools enrolling thirty-six percent of public school students in the district. "Never in a million years did I think we'd end up with [so many] charters in a community of this size," a former president of the Dayton board of education told a reporter in 2005. "We're developing two complete and competing public systems."[1]

Parents in South Philadelphia frustrated with their local school can choose to send their children to an independent public charter school on the other side of town, a science magnet school a short bus ride away, or a nearby for-profit Edison school that provides computers for each and every student. Of eighty-nine schools in New Orleans, fifty-two are charters that nearly 60 percent of the district's children attend.[2]

Because charter school founders receive the same funding per child that traditional public schools receive, issues of money and account-ability loom large. Champions of charters point out that they spend public dollars efficiently and get results; parents who send their children to charters hold the staffs accountable, advocates say.

Many critics, however, fear that the reform hurts public schools by drawing scarce funds away from the rest of the school system. More-over, states vary in their oversight of charter schools' academic per-formance. Other critics worry that putting market forces to work in a public system elevates the individual family's interests over the larger purposes served by tax-supported schools, such as developing good citi-zens, promoting shared social values, and equipping students with the skills to thrive in an ever-changing economy.

Where Did the Idea of Charter
Schools Originate?

Charters are part of a larger movement to expand parental choice of schools through vouchers, magnet schools, and other publicly financed options. Although parental choice attracted lots of attention in the early 1990s, its roots date back 150 years and are deeply embedded in demo-cratic principles. In the mid-nineteenth century, midwestern German parents got their school boards to establish schools that would conduct instruction in their native language. At about the same time, many urban Catholics wanted their schools to inculcate religious values and left public schools to establish private ones. In 1925, the U.S. Supreme Court prohibited states from requiring every student to attend public schools, thus making private schools and parental choice constitutional.[3]

By the 1960s and 1970s, liberals promoted parental choice through vouchers—or government-issued payments to cover tuition—because of their deep concern over ghetto-bound parents having to send their children to ineffective urban schools. Under some desegregation court orders, districts also established magnet schools focusing on special curricula where parents could choose to send their children instead of neighborhood schools. And in the mid-1990s, after Minnesota passed the first charter school law, both liberals and conservatives championed publicly funded forms of parental choice for both poor and middle-class families. Even at the height of this interest in choices for parents, well over 90 percent of American children still attended traditional public schools. Nonetheless, an established tradition of parental choice anchored in the law had emerged, with charters leading the pack among the nation's nearly ninety thousand public schools.

In 2010, nearly 5,000 charter schools enrolling 1.5 million students existed in every state and the District of Columbia. California had the most, with more than 800 charters serving almost 315,000 students; Texas was second with 480 charter campuses enrolling 115,000 students.[4] In 2009, more than 100 nonprofit education management companies (EMOs) in half of the states operated more than 600 public schools, most of them charters, with just over 180,000 students. For-profit EMOs (such as EdisonLearning) enrolled nearly 340,000 students.[5]

Parental choice is also embedded in NCLB. The law states that parents of students in failing schools can transfer to higher-performing schools or request tutoring from a private provider at school expense. Ultimately, if the school continues to fail, state officials can take over the school and outsource the school's management to a for-profit company, convert it into a charter school, or operate the school itself.[6]

What Problems Are Charters Intended to Solve?

Providing better options for parents whose children are trapped in lousy schools, stimulating innovation by freeing schools from the regulatory stranglehold of districts, and improving urban schools through competition are all problems that charter advocates claim to solve. Market-oriented reformers and business leaders believe public schools are an inefficient and ineffective monopoly that must be broken up. They promote charter schools as ways of freeing urban schools from their regulatory stranglehold and giving poor parents a chance to send their children to other, better schools. Moreover, injecting competition into both large and medium-sized urban districts from Los Angeles to Dayton (Ohio) gives parents choices among different options that would, proponents say, jolt boards of education and superintendents, fearful of losing students and state funds, into working harder to improve all urban schools.[7]

President Barack Obama and his secretary of education, Arne Duncan, believe that if more charters were available, poor parents would choose them. In the 2010 Race to the Top competition for $4.35 billion in federal stimulus funds, no ambiguity appeared in Duncan's words: "States that do not have public charter laws or put artificial caps on the growth of charter schools will jeopardize their applications under the Race to the Top Fund." At that time, ten states lacked charter school laws and twenty-six states had caps. Such restrictions, Duncan said, limited "choices for parents and students, and denying children access to new high-quality instruction." Federal policymakers seek to expand the pool of charter schools to broaden choices available to low-income families.[8]

As heated as the struggle over charter schools has been in the past decade, both promoters and opponents agree that parental involvement in their children's schooling increases the chances of their children doing better academically. Both sides also agree that large urban districts fail to offer poor parents the high-quality schooling that middle- and upper-income families secure when they buy homes in communities with strong public schools. Even with such agreement, conflicts over charters as a school reform will continue, particularly when the dollars to support such schools draw from the same purse that funds all public schools.

Do Charters Work?

One way to answer this question is to ask whether charters have increased the options available to poor parents. Parents in New York City,

Dayton, the District of Columbia, Philadelphia, Seattle, New Orleans, Milwaukee, and other places where charter schools are available do have more choices now. For most poor parents, however, the answer is no. In spite of the hullabaloo over choice-based options, less than 3 percent of all public schoolchildren attend these schools of choice as of 2010.

Another question to ask is whether charter schools are better options for parents than the urban schools they are designed to replace. Like urban schools, charters vary greatly—some are fine schools, others are dreadful—and many suffer from the same problems that beset urban districts. For example, in the last few years, Ohio's charter schools lost more than half their teachers, most of whom left teaching altogether. Of the 457 Arizona charter schools opened since 1997, 21 percent (96) have closed their doors.[9]

In terms of test scores, there is no clear winner. Some studies of charters claim that children do better in these schools, while other studies reject those claims and point out that students in public schools outscore those in charters. Dueling studies frustrate both parents and policymakers. Headlines such as "Charter Schools: Two Studies, Two Conclusions"—offering contradictory outcomes—give little confidence to those interested in whether these schools help, harm, or don't make a difference in student achievement. We do know that well-run education management organizations such as Knowledge Is Power Program (KIPP) boast charter schools that register higher test scores than regular schools enrolling similar students.[10]

Both charter advocates and opponents dispute the research design, sample selection, methodologies, and quality of the evidence of charter school studies. Depending on how much weight readers give to these technical issues, the mixed findings hardly bang the drums loudly for charter schools. For the immediate future, no clear answer to the question of whether charter schools are better than regular public schools can be found in research. But this question makes as much sense as asking whether all public schools work. A far better question to ask is, What makes some charters successful and others fail? Are KIPP charter schools successful because both students and teachers have chosen to embrace an ideology of academic success and participate fully in a range of practices—before, during, and after school—that create a tightly knit culture? Researchers need to ask such pointed questions of the small cadre of high-performing charter schools to understand the reasons behind their success.

Finally, have districts that established charter schools responded to the resulting competition by adopting new practices and raising levels of achievement? Here again, the evidence is mixed. Some researchers find increases in test scores in districts with many charter schools while others find the opposite, and some see no impact at all. Still others claim that charters themselves do not provide models of innovative practices but, rather, extensions of current practices (e.g., longer school days and academic afterschool programs), some of which have been picked up by districts.[11]

At best, then, the principle of choice and competition as advocated by charter school champions has yet to show persuasive evidence of unvarnished academic success or public school transformation. Of course, research and evaluation studies seldom determine the worth of a reform. Politics move policymakers and parents quicker and further than findings from researchers' investigations. The 1990 Minnesota charter school law triggered many states to legislate more of these schools. Federal funds underwriting The Race to the Top has led to even more enabling state legislation encouraging charter school growth.

The political popularity of charter schools as alternatives for minority students, teachers, and parents seeking customized options nearly guarantee that few elected officials will rescind legislation authorizing these choices. The ability of charters to expand on a large scale is much less certain. CMOs such as KIPP, Green Dot, Aspire, and Uncommon Schools rely on substantial philanthropic investment and cannot add more than a few schools each year to maintain the quality of their brand.[12] Political popularity does not solve these challenges.

The Solution, in Our View

Because charter schools serve a limited number of parents and show inconclusive results, solutions must follow two paths. One path is to continue to invest in improving the quality of urban schools, which still serve and will continue to serve the vast majority of children. Whatever their problems, it is unconscionable to turn away from attempting to strengthen these schools, no matter how hard the task or how slow the progress.

The second path is to ensure that charter schools operating with public money receive the same scrutiny, are held to the same standards, and provide the same safeguards against discriminatory practices as traditional public schools, including equal access regardless of language or disabling condition.[13] Charter schools that succeed offer a laboratory for learning what makes them tick and whether their ideas can work beyond schools where teachers choose to work and parents choose to send their children.

Regardless of the numbers or the research, charters and other choice options have staying power. Both tradition and court decisions preserve the rights of parents to send their children to charter schools or private schools or to homeschool them. Giving dissatisfied low-income parents schooling options that are superior to their neighborhood school is consistent with both tradition and democratic principles embedded in parental choice.

5

Performance-Based
Pay for Teachers

PAY-FOR-PERFORMANCE IS AS American as apple pie. Individuals who produce more earn more. Those who sell shoes, homes, and life insurance get paid commissions and bonuses on the basis of how much they sell. In commercial laundries, the number of shirts ironed determines how much pay the worker gets. Even doctors in a Minneapolis-based health plan receive bonuses if their diabetic patients get blood sugar and cholesterol below certain levels, stop smoking, and take aspirin daily. Business leaders and managers have known for decades that cash incentives can help motivate employees to perform at higher levels. Why not teachers?[1]

For every year a teacher teaches, she gets an incremental raise. If she earns an advanced degree or a certificate for a teaching specialty, she receives another increase. After fifteen or twenty years, teachers top out in most district salary schedules, except for occasional small longevity increases marking twenty-five and thirty years of service.

Such salary plans prize experience and university coursework. A predictable salary schedule allows teachers to plan for the future and provides a degree of security. Moreover, a uniform schedule avoids pitting teacher against teacher in seeking favor with administrators who evaluate their performance; it encourages teachers to cooperate, rather than compete, with one another.

Uniform salary schedules also have a downside. The system of compensation assumes that all teachers are equally effective. It provides no incentive for teachers to reach beyond their grasp or to innovate, since all teachers—mediocre and high performing—are paid the same as long as they exceed the threshold of acceptable classroom performance. Perversely, a uniform schedule encourages experienced, effective teachers to transfer out of low-performing, largely minority schools where workplace conditions are difficult to affluent schools where teaching conditions are more attractive, and yet they receive the same salary they earned at the tougher school.

Thus, performance-based pay plans—paying teachers for results—appeal to policymakers looking to reward effective teachers and to penalize slackers and inadequate teaching. Reformers view performance pay as a way to motivate individual teachers to excel and to encourage or require those who are inadequate to leave the profession. The rub lies in how effective teaching is defined and measured.

Where Did the Idea of Performance Pay Originate?

In the early twentieth century, teachers received whatever school boards decided to pay them. Salaries were set arbitrarily and often depended on personal contacts, not classroom performance or how much students learned. Because there was little predictability or fairness in such an arbitrary system of compensation, school reformers, seeking to provide security to teachers in an emerging profession, introduced the uniform salary schedule in the 1920s.

Since then, nearly all teachers have been paid on schedules that rewarded experience and credentials, not performance. Pay-for-performance plans have emerged frequently in the past half-century, particularly in moments of growing dissatisfaction with public schools for producing inadequate high school graduates. During the cold war, for example, the Soviet Union's launch of the satellite Sputnik in 1957 prompted critics to lambaste U.S. public schools for failing to produce more engineers, mathematicians, and scientists than their rival. Among the many post-Sputnik school reforms adopted was merit, or performance-based, pay for teachers. About 10 percent of school districts in the nation embraced such plans. Within a few years, however, most had dropped them.[2]

In the past decade, mounting public displeasure with low-performing schools, especially in big cities, led critics to borrow business practices and press for teacher performance pay plans. The Obama administration has continued the former Bush administration policies that push for "reforming teacher and principal compensation systems so that teachers and principals are rewarded for increases in student achievement."[3] In 2009, states and districts had to promise to link teacher evaluation and pay to student test scores if they wanted to compete for almost $5 billion in Race to the Top and Teacher Incentive Fund grants.

A growing number of states and districts have adopted various performance-pay plans believing they will motivate teachers either to improve or to leave the profession. By 2009, eleven states had adopted performance pay programs, including Georgia and Texas, and twenty-six states had districts with such plans. More will follow to ensure a chance at pulling in large federal grants. Local performance pay plans rewarding individuals and groups of teachers for improving student achievement have been launched in Chattanooga, Houston, Minneapolis, and Denver. New York's mayor Michael Bloomberg announced in the fall of 2009 that the public school system would immediately incorporate student test scores in decisions about teacher tenure, and the District of Columbia's chancellor and the teacher union agreed to a pilot program in 2010.

Not everyone is on board, however. States applying for Race to the Top grants have not convinced all their districts that commitments to performance-based pay are worth making. In Illinois and California, fewer than half the districts have agreed to participate.[4]

Teacher unions have stood on both sides of the pay-for-performance question, either endorsing or opposing plans that linked student test scores to compensation. Denver's plan, called ProComp, was initiated by the school board and superintendent, developed in close cooperation with the teacher union, and begun as an experiment in 1999. It gained the support of most Denver teachers, and subsequently, in 2005, city voters approved a tax referendum to support it.

PERFORMANCE PAY: THE DENVER STORY

In 2004, the Denver Classroom Teachers Association voted to dump a traditional salary schedule based on years of experience and college credits and to endorse a new merit pay plan that includes bonuses for teachers who raise students' test scores. Shortly afterward, a mayor-led coalition of civic, business, and educational leaders spent more than $1 million to promote a ballot measure to underwrite—at a cost of $25 million—a pay plan called ProComp. The measure passed in the fall of 2005.

So, how did this uncommon civic, business, and educator partnership succeed where others have failed?

The answer can be found in joint leadership and planning, much patience, and attention to teacher concerns. Teacher union leaders worked closely with top school officials for six years. With the help of private funding and careful planning, the union and administration agreed to a four-year pilot project incorporating elements of pay-for-performance in sixteen of the district's 130-plus schools. Most teachers who participated in the pilot have earned $1,500 for meeting performance objectives they had set. Teachers and administrators analyzed glitches that left some teachers angry and a revised Professional Compensation System for Teachers, or ProComp, emerged with a two-year implementation beginning in 2006.

ProComp offers teachers a menu of choices. They can earn additional money—a percentage of the starting yearly pay for a credentialed teacher (almost $33,000)—by acquiring new skills and knowledge in their teaching field, receiving satisfactory evaluations, demonstrating growth in student achievement, or working in schools with children from poor families. Current teachers have six years to decide whether to join ProComp; new teachers enter the plan automatically.

For ten-year veteran math teacher Taylor Betz, who works at a low-income middle school earning just over $45,000 a year, Pro-Comp offers a financial incentive. Under the current salary schedule, her annual pay increases would end after thirteen years, except for small bumps every five years. At that rate, after thirty years of teaching, she would be making $57,190. Should she join ProComp, however, and continue to teach math in a low-income school, gather professional development credits for courses, and meet her annual goals, she could collect $3,000 to $4,000 in yearly increases, taking her up to $100,000 in salary after thirty years.

"Teachers doing hard work in the hardest places deserve to be rewarded," Betz told *Teacher Magazine* in 2004, though she was quick to add that the money wasn't what motivated her. "I've chosen to do this regardless of pay," she said.

In 2008, the union and Denver administration agreed on a new contract extending performance pay. Denver teachers approved the contract endorsing ProComp while adding new incentives and resolving items that had been in dispute.

SOURCES

Brown, Cynthia, and Robin Chait. "A Promising Accord for Denver's ProComp Program." Issue Alerts: Center for American Progress, September 2, 2008. http://www.americanprogress.org/issues/2008/09/procomp_denver.html.

Keller, Bess. "Teacher Vote on Merit Pay Down to Wire." *Education Week*, March 17, 2004, 1, 22–23.

———. "Denver Teachers Approve Pay-for-Performance Plan." *Education Week,* March 23, 2004. www.edweek.org/ew/articles/2004/03/23/28denver_web.h23.html.

Meyers, Kerby. "Performance Anxiety." *Teacher Magazine,* November 2004, 15–19.

In 2004 New York City and the state of California, where the mayor and governor, respectively, proposed performance pay, teacher unions in both places quickly took out ads opposing the plans.[5] However, in early 2010, the president of the New York City teacher union and its parent organization announced a willingness to incorporate student test scores in teacher evaluations.[6]

What Problem Is Performance-Based Pay Intended to Solve?

The prevailing assumption that more money will motivate teachers to teach better and thereby produce increased student learning is widely shared among policymakers of all political persuasions. Policymakers also believe that the performance evaluations on which pay is based can lead to dismissing teachers who are not performing up to snuff. Pushing for a state referendum for performance pay, California governor Arnold Schwarzenegger said in his 2005 "State of the State Address":

> [For] $50 billion [in the budget] . . . we still have 30 percent of high school students not graduating. That is a human disaster. Fifty billion dollars and we still have hundreds of schools that are failing. That is an institutional disaster. Fifty billion dollars and the majority of our students cannot even perform at their grade level. That is an educational disaster. We must reward— we must financially reward—good teachers and expel those who are not. The more we reward excellent teachers, the more our teachers will be excellent. The more we tolerate ineffective teachers, the more our teachers will be ineffective. So . . .
> I propose that a teacher's pay be tied to merit, not tenure. And I propose that a teacher's employment be tied to performance, not just showing up.[7]

In 2009, the District of Columbia's school chancellor, Michelle Rhee, echoed similar sentiments: "You have to be able to evaluate teachers based on their effectiveness in obtaining gains in student achievement and then make the determination about whether they should continue to be employed by the district based on whether or not they are producing results for kids."[8]

Like the governor and the D.C. chancellor, advocates believe that performance pay will eliminate a salary schedule that rewards longevity, protects mediocre teachers, and denies effective teachers their due recognition. Second, they say it will attract better teachers, spur on teachers to improve, and, as a result, raise the performance of their students and, ultimately, underperforming American schools. Advocates are also convinced that so-called "value-added" test score measures can solve technical problems of the past, thereby making comparisons among teachers more fair.[9]

Does Performance-Based Pay Work?

Little historical or contemporary evidence exists that the basic assumption driving performance-based pay systems will hold up in practice. For example, paying teachers for student performance on tests did not work in late-nineteenth-century Great Britain when Parliament mandated it. In its more than three decades in practice there, many problems arose, including improper allocation of funds, widespread cheating, and constricted forms of teaching, which led to the British system's demise in 1897.[10]

In the United States since the 1920s, most performance-based pay plans in public schools were enthusiastically adopted but disappeared within a few years. If such plans cannot survive more than a few years, they are unlikely to produce the intended benefits. Although teacher unions are often cast as the nay-sayers, the reasons for adoption or disappearance seldom had to do with the position the unions took. After all, in examining private schools where few unions exist, researchers found few performance-based compensation plans. Moreover, advocates attack tenure as if it is only a union demand when in fact all states have laws that confer tenure on teachers after their probationary period—laws designed to protect teachers from arbitrary or capricious firing by their superiors.

In public schools, some performance pay plans have lasted decades, but they have been transformed. Usually what began as bonuses for better teaching or improved test scores morphed into extra pay for extra work, or spreading small payments across large numbers of teachers to gain greater participation and legitimacy. Or the money simply ran out. Historically, paying teachers more for better teaching has, at best, a bleak record.

Why has performance-based pay contained such lethal genes? The answer lies in a simple but powerful question always asked by teachers and rarely by administrators and policymakers: Why did that teacher get a bonus and I didn't? And there's the rub. What is the basis for judging whether one teacher is more effective than another? Bonuses are not likely to motivate teachers to improve if they are based on measures perceived to be biased, unfair, or capricious.

In the past, most performance pay plans have been based on traditional evaluations of teachers, on supervisor judgments. Unlike ironing shirts, selling houses, or fastening chips to a motherboard, however, teaching is not piecework and cannot be readily counted. No checklist can objectively capture "good" teaching. (We place the word "good" in quotation marks to acknowledge that there are many forms of effective teaching, not just one.)

Consider why such a checklist is hard to compile. Teachers know that success with students depends on their subject knowledge, skills, and awareness of students' background as displayed through classroom interactions. Teachers know that family background plays an important part in determining students' motivation and work behavior and what they learn. Finally, teachers know from experience that others (e.g., principals, parents, students, other teachers, taxpayers) have their own ideas of "good" teaching, including those officials who end up evaluating the quality of their teaching. All of these factors can influence what the teacher does after she closes the classroom door.

Although no single checklist recognizing all the factors influencing teaching and learning exists, most educators would agree that the basic ingredients of effectiveness are well-prepared lessons, active engagement of students in those lessons through a variety of teaching methods, monitoring academic progress, and managing behavior. Yet these ingredients do not translate into a surefire formula for "good" teaching.

Business leaders and policymakers promote reliance on student test scores to avoid the subjectivity of supervisor ratings and to provide a seemingly objective number. If students learn more in some teachers' classes than others based on their test score increases from one year to the next, then, advocates argue, these teachers deserve more pay. Teachers are not alone in their hue and cry over this approach. Statisticians and economists argue over whether it is possible to figure out how much of test score gains are due to the teacher as opposed to the students and other factors beyond the control of the teacher. Most agree that even the fanciest statistical techniques are only good enough to identify the very best and the very worst teachers. Principals, teachers, and even parents can do this.

If judgments that form the basis for salary bonuses are not deemed reasonable and fair, the system will self-destruct. If teachers known to be loafers receive bonuses, performance pay is doomed. If excellent teachers who have spoken out in faculty meetings or questioned administrators are denied bonuses, performance pay has little chance of gaining legitimacy among teachers. Unfortunately, few performance-based pay plans convince the very people they are supposed to motivate that the process is fair and untainted by personal favor or factors beyond the control of the teacher.

Few pay-for-performance systems survive long enough to judge whether they have their intended effect on the teaching force. For not only do the plans need to pass muster with the profession, they need funding. When budgets get tight, money that is not locked into the salary schedule goes by the wayside. Teachers are well aware of this history, which further fuels their skepticism about the lifespan of such plans.

The Solution, in Our View

If performance-based pay plans are designed with little concern for teachers' sense of fairness and legitimacy, the lethal genes described above will guarantee an early death. However, that need not be the case every time compensation for performance is proposed. Many teachers yearn for a fair process of rewarding excellence in teaching and improved student learning. A 2010 study found that most teachers support frequent observations by their principals as well as measures of how much their students are engaged and how much they learn compared to other students.[11]

Yet, when the focus is on getting rid of teachers, rather than strengthening the profession, backlash is predictable. When Houston's school board approved a policy allowing the firing of teachers whose students fall short on standardized tests, parents cheered and teachers booed.[12] The Obama administration's focus on incentives for good teachers to go to bad schools and the Gates Foundation's focus on developing measures of teacher effectiveness that identify which teachers need support could create a less punitive atmosphere: "A new [teacher evaluation] system needs to be predictable and help teachers identify weaknesses and give them ways to improve, and it should not make capable teachers afraid of capricious results . . . A better system should certainly identify the small minority who don't belong in teaching, but its key benefit is that it will help most teachers improve."[13]

Teachers want plans that answer their questions and give serious consideration to the issues they raise about pay for performance. Serious and sustained involvement of teachers at the very beginning of discussions about incentive pay plans is a necessary (but not sufficient) condition. Performance pay is no magic bullet. Removing ineffective teachers helps only if more qualified teachers are in line. Attracting better teachers to low-performing schools works only if they stay; without support and a congenial environment, financial incentives are not enough.[14]

When teachers have a say in the goals that are set and the measures used to judge teaching performance, and when they can choose from an array of opportunities (e.g., mentoring new teachers, developing curriculum and assessments, teaching demonstration lessons) to reach those agreed-on goals, then that involvement lends a legitimacy to performance pay that has been missing for decades. The Denver experience with ProComp, the Chattanooga plan of professional development and awarding bonuses to teachers who not only volunteer to teach in high-poverty schools but also raise students' test scores, and programs in a few other districts have taken seriously teacher involvement in designing performance pay systems. Plans such as these promise positive outcomes for teachers, students, and the larger community.

6

Putting Urban
Mayors in Charge

"I F READING AND math scores aren't significantly higher, I will look in the mirror and say I've failed." A reasonable guess as to who said this in 2002 would be a superintendent of schools. Actually, it was New York City mayor Michael Bloomberg, who then went on to say, "I have never failed at anything in my life." A few years earlier, Boston mayor Tom Menino, standing on the steps of a high school denied accreditation, said to the city's voters, "I want to be judged as your mayor by what happens now in the Boston Public Schools. I expect you to hold me accountable . . . If I fail, judge me harshly." In 2010, voters held both mayors accountable and reelected them.[1]

New York City and Boston are not exceptions. Since the mid-1990s, Chicago, Cleveland, Philadelphia, Detroit, and the District of Columbia have seen their mayors deeply engaged in shaping the school district or actually appointing the superintendent. Other mayors, in Hartford, Connecticut, and elsewhere, who have had little direct influence on their cities' school boards have appointed more board members in an effort to shape school policies. Big-city mayors have, at best, only an indirect influence on schools, much less on classroom teaching. So why are they betting their political futures on improving students' academic performance?

Where Did the Idea Originate?

A century ago, good-government urban reformers changed their city charters to separate public schools from mayoral control. They were angered and sickened by the many mayors who had assembled political machines and appointed cronies to run city police, fire, sanitation, and other departments, including the schools. Mayors frequently appointed political hacks to school boards that then handed out teacher and principal jobs to machine supporters like turkeys at holiday time. Mayors looked on schools, sanitation, police, and fire departments as employment bureaus. Reformers wanted independently elected school boards and a firewall between these boards and mayors to put schools out of the reach of city politics. By the 1920s, progressive reformers had succeeded in sealing off schools from mayoral influence by establishing nonpartisan elected school boards and civil service exams to screen out unqualified job seekers. Most cities (except for a few, such as Chicago and Baltimore) elected mayors who kept their hands off boards of education.

In the decades following World War II, however, demography altered major cities. After four years of war, white, middle-class families living in cities wanted a patch of lawn, more space for their children to play, and larger homes in the suburbs. At the same time, immigrants, the poor, and minorities swept into cities seeking cheap housing and jobs. Slums, crime, increasing racial conflict, and periodic unemployment accelerated the exodus of middle-class families and caused businesses and industry to move away from cities to places with lower taxes and less crime, thereby drawing taxable wealth and jobs from cities. Less tax revenue meant urban schools received less funding, even though the needs of low-income minority children for additional services in and out of schools escalated. Student academic performance got worse; more high school students dropped out before graduating.

Although parents, business leaders, and civic elites looked to schools as the linchpin in a city's economic success, many urban boards of education and their superintendents openly squabbled with one another, making the school chief's job like a revolving door. School boards could not reverse the downward spiral of community poverty and crime, high dropout rates, and low academic achievement. So in a number of cities, elected mayors, fearing impending economic disaster, intervened.

What Problem Is Mayoral
Control Intended to Solve?

Since the 1970s, most urban school boards were impotent, with dismal records of one failed reform after another and zero accountability. Anxious to revive their cities economically and culturally, business leaders, state officials, parents, and civic elites in the 1990s pushed for changes in city charters to give mayors responsibility for what happens in schools. When mayors take control of the school district, authority for governing schools shifts from nonpartisan elected school boards to a Republican or Democratic city hall. The mayor, or a board appointed by the mayor, selects the superintendent. A mayor can mobilize citywide campaigns to support schools. A mayor can use more city resources (e.g., housing, employment, police, recreation, social services) to help schools. And if a mayor fails, voters can boot him or her out of office.

In Chicago, Cleveland, Boston, New York, and Washington, D.C., mayors appoint both school boards and the schools' superintendent (or, in some cities, CEO or chancellor). Boston voters, for example, passed a referendum in 1992 ending the elected school committee that had governed schools for decades and giving Mayor Menino the authority to appoint a school committee and superintendent. The prevailing belief among these city's civic and business leaders—that poor school performance was rooted in defective school board policies—led to the same solution: a dramatic change in governance that would reverse shabby academic performance.[2]

Does Mayoral Control Work?

Some results of mayoral control are evident. Familiar conflicts between elected boards and their superintendents amplified in the media seldom occur when mayors appoint top school officials. In most cases, mayoral control of the school system has led to centralized decision making by the superintendents and their deputies. Business and civic elites gain more influence over schools since newly appointed board members are often drawn from mayor-friendly groups. Schools are able to more easily offer the services of once-separate city departments to their students and families (e.g., community centers, child care, recreation, social services).

At the same time, however, mayor-appointed boards are more removed from constituents. No longer is there a monthly public forum to debate school policy, and, as a result, public participation in school district decisions shrinks.[3]

But do these changes in governance improve academic performance, the primary reason for the reform? The evidence, at best, is mixed. Over the past few years in some mayoral control cities (New York, Boston, Chicago, Cleveland), elementary school test scores have seen modest increases, though secondary schools have registered hardly any change. In Detroit, test scores have fallen across the board. Gaps in test scores between white and minority students have narrowed in some places where mayors control schools but widened in others. There is no pattern of school success that can be attributed to shifting policy-making responsibility from elected school boards to mayors.[4]

Two reasons might explain the absence of any pattern. First, there are no recipes for improving test scores that mayors can hand over to competent educators. Appointing an outside superstar superintendent, business executive, or corporate lawyer is, at best, a mere beginning. Improving teaching and learning requires connecting the many links—the mayor, the appointed school board, the superintendent, central office, principals, teachers, and, ultimately, the students. It takes hard work and ample resources invested in schools, a stable and experienced teaching staff, and sustained support for teachers and principals. Simply ordering educators to do better may make for catchy newspaper headlines—Mayor Bloomberg said "there is a direct link from the teacher's desk in the classroom, right to the mayor's desk in City Hall"—but mayoral influence does not reach a teacher after she closes the classroom door. So while moving political control from an elected school board to the mayor shifts power to hire and fire superintendents, it does not necessarily make much difference in running schools or teaching students.[5]

Second, a mayor's time for schools is limited by competing electoral concerns over poverty, homelessness, the tax base, crime, and public health, to mention only a few issues. Because school improvement takes far more time—anywhere from five to ten years—than the common four-year electoral cycle, mayors must prove to voters that they have succeeded. That is hard to do with schools that need a lot of time and help in order to demonstrate success. Further, when a mayor leaves office, the educational agenda may well shift—for better or worse.

For these reasons, governance change may be a popular mechanism, but it is severely limited in its ability to alter classroom practice and improve students' academic performance. "Taking over a school system," Columbus (Ohio) mayor Michael Coleman said in 2003, "is not synonymous with an improved school system."[6]

The Solution, in Our View

Mayoral control may work in some cities, but not in others. Boston voters abolished their elected school board because it failed to improve schools and its conflicts with superintendents became a chronic embarrassment. Voters wanted mayoral control over the schools. Austin, Texas, to cite a counterexample, has traditional school board–superintendent governance. The mayor and city manager largely avoided the turmoil plaguing that district's schools in the 1990s. The Austin schools recovered in the following decade without mayoral intervention. Simply put, governance change in and of itself does not necessarily make better schools.

In some cities, elected school boards have lost their way in trying to improve schools, while other urban elected school boards have succeeded in slowly improving their schools. Austin, Seattle, Cincinnati, Minneapolis, Denver, and Sacramento, among many other urban districts wrestling with lack of resources, poor neighborhoods, teacher mobility, and other serious issues, have used traditional governance to work toward school improvement. These school boards hired superintendents who held administrators accountable for student performance, expanded preschools, built instructional support systems for teachers and principals, and reported steady gains in elementary school scores. These school boards recognized that sustained support for change is an essential condition as they press forward with secondary school agendas, recruiting qualified teachers, establishing small high schools, and focusing on instructional improvement.

In short, nothing miraculous resides in mayoral control, traditional school board governance, or hybrids of each. What matters is local context, leadership, and political will.

7

New Pathways to Teaching

IT'S NO SECRET that schools and classrooms with the most challenging teaching situations lose out in getting good teachers and principals who stick around for more than a year or two. Like "a chicken in every pot," No Child Left Behind's "a highly qualified teacher in every classroom" is just a slogan, but it does highlight the need to attract and train good teachers who are willing to take on these challenging situations.

In the last couple of decades, new players have appeared on the teacher preparation landscape that was dominated in the past by universities. These newcomers offer programs designed specifically to prepare teachers for jobs in low-performing urban schools and hard-to-staff areas, including math, science, and special education. Proponents argue that traditional training programs take too long and require courses that are not relevant or useful. They believe they can get the job done: attract and train a broader range of prospective teachers and get them quickly into classrooms where they are most needed. Critics claim that the new programs give short shrift to vital coursework that helps teachers understand how students learn and effective ways to teach particular subjects. Taking on full-time teaching responsibilities with minimal preparation and oversight, they say, sets up new teachers for failure. Critics wonder, Would citizens support analogous programs for meeting the shortage of nurses?

But these are broad brush strokes. In fact, new pathways to teaching come in many shapes and forms. Some offer programs quite similar to traditional university-based credentialing programs; others provide shortcuts to place teachers in understaffed classrooms quickly. Some are partnerships that include universities and school districts; others are independent organizations, state agencies, or districts themselves. What they do varies from program to program: for example, the amount and kind of coursework, how quickly prospective teachers are placed in classrooms, and whether candidates are student teachers with close supervision or the fulltime teacher of record.

Still, debates rage over how much can be learned from coursework versus on the job, as well as over what teachers really need to know to be effective. The bottom-line question is, Do these new pathways actually increase the number of qualified teachers in hard-to-staff schools and classrooms?

Where Did the Idea for New Pathways to Teaching Originate?

In the 1960s, urban districts were desperate for new teachers, largely because few graduates of traditional teacher education programs were choosing to teach in their schools. With federal funding under the Johnson administration's "War on Poverty," programs like the National Teacher Corps recruited returning Peace Corps volunteers and recent college graduates to teach in urban schools. Designed to facilitate entry into teaching for those without education training, these programs attracted college graduates who agreed to teach low-income students in inner-city and rural schools in exchange for stipends and tuition. These programs were expensive to operate, however, since they paid the interns and hired master teachers to work with them. Thus, by the early 1980s, few such programs remained.[1]

By the end of the 1980s, teacher vacancies had skyrocketed in high-poverty urban schools, topping 20 percent annually. With new teachers hard to find, substitute teachers too often filled the positions.[2] These chronically high vacancy rates provided an impetus for expanding the types and number of alternative paths to attract teachers to urban schools. These new pathways also responded to the perceived need to create less costly and speedier paths into teaching, both for college graduates who did not major in education and for those seeking midcareer changes. More recently, the many references to "qualified teachers" in No Child Left Behind and newly targeted federal support for teacher training have further stimulated the development and expansion of new pathways to teaching.

The last two decades brought 125 new routes to become a certified teacher, totaling roughly six hundred programs that exist outside traditional university-based teacher education. These programs, like traditional teacher education programs, vary considerably. They range from intensive master degree programs with coursework followed by year-long apprenticeships under master teachers to fast-track programs that provide a modicum of preparation and then put teachers in full charge of classrooms.

In 2006, these programs together produced nearly sixty thousand teachers nationally across all fifty states.[3] In New Jersey, Texas, and California, one-third of all new hires come through alternate certification programs.[4] And they continue to expand. In 1990 Teach for America (TFA) recruited five hundred college graduates; by 2010, TFA had 7,300 first- and second-year teachers in one hundred school districts in twenty-seven states and the District of Columbia.

These alternate paths have tapped completely different populations in recruiting new teachers.[5] TFA, for example, recruits graduates from elite universities to teach for two years in urban schools. Similar programs such as the New Teacher Project, which offers recruitment services to districts as well as training, have introduced college graduates from top universities and midcareer professionals from business, law, and the military into schools. Although these new pathways increasingly compete with traditional teacher education institutions for positions in urban school districts, their programs fill only a fraction of teacher vacancies.[6]

EXAMPLES OF DIFFERENT PATHWAYS TO TEACHING

Traditional university undergraduate education program. Still the most common approach, students take courses in education departments and relevant subject areas and earn a certificate when they get their bachelor's degree. Some student teaching is required.

Master of Arts in Teaching (MAT). Students take graduate-level coursework combined with some type of classroom teaching experience. Like undergraduate programs, coursework and practical experience vary.

New Teacher Project (NTP) and Teach for America (TFA). These alternative programs recruit primarily midcareer changers (NTP) and elite college graduates (TFA) and place them in high-poverty schools. Both provide a summer "boot camp" prior to full-time teaching and some mentoring during their teaching commitment (two years for TFA). Both expect teachers to enroll in a teacher credentialing program while teaching, usually done through a local university.

Urban teacher residency (UTR). Relatively new and supported largely by federal grants, this pathway is typically a partnership between an urban district, a university, and a nonprofit. Candidates take classes in the summer and during the school year (typically one day a week) and spend the school year working alongside a

What Problem Is New Pathways Intended to Solve?

High-poverty schools, both urban and rural, struggle to attract good teachers and keep them for more than a year or two. New pathways aim to get good teachers into hard-to-staff schools and subjects quickly. Even during times when teacher vacancies are at a relative low, as in the current recession, high turnover continues in the poorest urban and rural schools. And schools, especially urban and rural, are always trained mentor teacher in a high-poverty school, often as part of team of residents and mentors. Residents receive stipends and/or loans that are forgiven in exchange for a commitment to teach in urban schools for several years.

New Jersey's Provisional Teacher program. The first statewide alternative certification program, it was designed to streamline access to teaching, especially for career changers. Prerequisites include a bachelor's degree with a minimum GPA of 2.75; a major in the subject if secondary school; and a passing score on a national teacher exam. Prospective teachers get a provisional license, enroll in a program offered by regional training centers (usually operated by universities), and pay for mentoring (full time during their first twenty days of teaching and continued part-time support for the rest of the year.

SOURCES

Humphrey, Daniel C., Marjorie E. Wechsler, and Heather J. Hough. "Characteristics of Effective Alternative Teacher Certification Programs." *Teachers College Record* 110, no. 1 (2008): 1–63.

Paulson, Amanda. "Teacher Training: What's the Best Way?" *Christian Science Monitor,* March 27, 2009.

on the lookout for teachers in subjects that are traditionally hard to staff —math, science, and special education. Advocates for alternative routes also seek to attract a more diverse group of applicants including more males, minorities, and older candidates.

Do New Pathways Work?

That these new pathway programs recruit a different population into teaching is clear.[7] From elite college graduates to midcareer professionals, new pathways have successfully attracted prospective teachers who were unlikely to enroll in traditional teacher-training institutions.

Much less clear is whether new pathways produce teachers who are as effective as those who are traditionally trained. Given the broad range of both alternative and traditional programs, it hardly makes sense to lump them all together to ask whether alternative or traditional programs produce better teachers, not to mention the difficulty in getting agreement on how to measure teacher effectiveness. Researchers find that, like some traditional programs, some alternative pathways have very small effects on student achievement and classroom practices.[8] Moreover, even within the same training model, both program features and teacher effectiveness as measured by student achievement can be quite different.[9]

Researchers concur on one universal finding: rookie teachers (those in their first three years) do not do as well as they would with more experience.[10] The constant turnover of teachers in high-poverty schools has been a major impetus for the development of new pathways that target these schools. So, one way to judge whether new pathways work is to look at teacher retention. Do teachers from alternative programs stick around?

For programs like TFA that attract the best and the brightest into high-poverty schools for two years, the answer is clear: the majority leave the classroom by the end of two years or sooner.[11] Some programs are too new to have retention data. Others show some evidence of higher retention rates but do not have data on effectiveness.[12] We do know, however, that the overall attrition rate among teachers in the first five years of service remains about the same, approaching 50 percent in high-poverty schools.

The Solution, in Our View

We know with certainty that there is no one best way to prepare teachers. Although most agree that some combination of coursework and supervised on-the-ground experience and knowledge of the subjects to be taught are important, a wide range of possible approaches remain.

Increasing the likelihood that prospective teachers will be effective and stick with teaching in high-poverty schools is a national challenge. A benefit of debates about traditional versus new pathways to teaching has been renewed interest in strengthening teacher preparation across all of them. One result is the emergence of new models that blend the old and the new. For example, the federal government has recently invested millions of dollars in "residency programs," which are often partnerships between an urban district, a degree-granting university, and an intermediary organization. Such models include extensive coursework with a year of working on a school team without classroom responsibility followed by a year or more of intensive mentoring while teaching part or fulltime.

Given the variety of programs in both traditional and alternative pathways to teaching, it is especially important to increase support for research that digs into which features of programs seem to make the most difference in teacher effectiveness and retention, whether traditional or alternative. As pathways expand and combine familiar features in new ways, such studies offer more promise for policy guidance than futile research designs comparing traditional and nontraditional programs that do little more than fuel unproductive arguments.

Still, teacher preparation can go only so far. The real solution lies in what happens after teachers complete their program, whether it is traditional or nontraditional or something in-between. We know that it is the first few years *after* completion of preparation programs that matters most in determining whether a teacher stays or exits.

Post-program support is, of course, expensive, as are the most intensive preparation programs, such as the residency model. Without such support, the high teacher attrition rate in the poorest schools will continue. Support means more than an occasional mentor visit; it means investment in creating the kinds of workplace conditions—from books to a collegial environment—that support teachers in difficult teaching situations. Yet this piece is missing when policymakers discuss and decide how to get more effective teachers into classrooms.

PART TWO

Reforming How Schools Are Organized

In this section, we focus on the keystone organization in K–12 education: the age-graded school. Developed in the mid–nineteenth century to remedy the inefficiencies of one-room schoolhouses, the age-graded school remains the norm. And, while the system reforms described in the previous section turn on changes in the ways schools are organized, reform proposals generally view the age-graded school as a given.

The reforms we discuss here include whether to hold back failing students, the size of classes, and changing the school calendar and schedule. Similarly, we address borrowing best practices from other schools, strategies for transforming the lowest-performing schools, and leading instructional change. We also look at breaking up large urban high schools and eliminating ability groupings.

8

Ending Social
Promotion

LESTER FINISHES THIRD grade still struggling to read sentences without stumbling over several words. He doesn't like to read, but he does enjoy addition and subtraction, although, again, he works slowly and does not yet understand multiplication. His test scores on a typical timed standardized test are well below the fiftieth percentile, the national average. Still, he listens to the teacher and does his work. Should Lester advance to the fourth grade?

"No more social promotion!" has become a reform rallying cry, particularly in large urban districts faced with thousands of struggling students like Lester. Critics of social promotion believe students should not advance to the next grade in the face of evidence that they have not successfully met the school's criteria for their current grade. Who could disagree with ending this seemingly illogical practice? A student who doesn't have the knowledge and skills to succeed in third grade will surely not be able to succeed in fourth grade. And the fourth-grade teacher will face students unprepared to tackle grade-level work. If ending social promotion makes so much sense, why not do it everywhere?

A closer look, however, raises some tough questions: How are "passing" and "failing" determined? What happens to students who are held back? Do better alternatives than social promotion exist to help students who fall behind?

Where Did the Idea Originate?

Social promotion happens because our system of schools is age-graded, with students moving through school according to age: you are six in first grade, seven in second grade, and so on. The United States borrowed this idea from mid-nineteenth-century Prussia. In the late nineteenth century, however, most American students left school by the fourth or fifth grade and went to work. Only a handful ever attended high school. Reformers in the early twentieth century introduced kindergarten in order to bring students into public school earlier and junior high schools in order to keep them there longer. They pushed through compulsory school attendance laws and legislation prohibiting child labor. By the 1930s, influenced by the Great Depression, millions of students were staying in school longer, and nearly half of all students were receiving high school diplomas.

As public schooling through high school became common, however, school boards and superintendents faced a new problem. Many students couldn't keep up and were held back, but retaining large numbers of students meant that too many older students congregated in the lower grades. As a result, in the 1930s educators came up with the idea of social promotion as a solution to this "pile-up" problem. Most school boards defined passing a grade by the number of failures the organization could tolerate—usually less than 5 percent of the students in a grade. Since students are expected to move up a grade each year, formal or informal policies usually define passing in a way that ends up promoting most students. And that's what has happened in public schools today. Most students are moved to the next grade, ready or not, leaving room for the incoming class of students.

Of course, school boards in the 1930s and 1940s could have spent lots of money helping students catch up with their age-mates. Or administrators could have intervened in the early grades when academic troubles first surfaced. Both would have reduced social promotions considerably. But at the time, the money simply wasn't there. When money did become available in later years, summer school emerged as the second-chance option for failing students.

What Problem Is Banning Social Promotion Intended to Solve?

Ending social promotion is supposed to stop the practice of pushing students through school when they are not yet equipped to learn at a higher level. It's a problem with serious consequences for individual students who fail to learn and, at the institutional level, for schools and universities as well as for employers who must teach these graduates what they have missed. When students graduate from high school without knowing how to read or write, politicians blame social promotion.

In today's high-stakes accountability climate, ending social promotion is also intended to motivate students to work harder. The argument is that if students know they will not move to the next grade unless they pass a test, they will be inspired to work harder to avoid being held back. As a result, more students will earn a passing grade and the number retained will be smaller. For those who do not pass the test, second chances are often available in retaking the test and summer school.

Under the current wave of standards-based reform, a ban on social promotion implicitly tackles a perennial problem faced by teachers: how to decide whether to promote particular students. Educators worry about which factors to weigh and the best balance among such things as grades, test scores, and behavior. Should the teachers promote an elementary school student who reads well but is failing math, or a student who has made substantial progress but started school far behind his peers, or a student who is well behaved and works hard but makes little progress?

Today, if a teacher's district prohibits social promotion, he may have little or no voice in deciding whether a child is ready for the next grade. Prodded by NCLB, most urban districts are turning to test scores as the primary, if not sole, criterion for passing. This may make the decision simpler for the teacher but less appropriate for the student whose particular strengths and needs are no longer taken into account.

There is also the problem of setting the cutoff test score that will define promotion or retention. There is no guarantee that a test-based standard will keep the number of failures relatively small, particularly if the cutoff score is tied to national averages. In Chicago, the policy begun in 1996 to end social promotion resulted in one-third of the students failing to make the test score cutoffs. Fortunately, summer school provided a second chance for many of the students, especially those from higher-performing schools.[1]

Does Banning Social Promotion Work?

Today, many students, averaging 13 percent overall and ranging as high as 50 percent for black males, are held back, and rates have increased since 1970.[2] Yet research on retention has turned up few positive results for individual students. These youngsters are more likely to continue their record of poor achievement and more likely to drop out of school than their peers who have been promoted.[3] In fact, retention turns out to be the strongest predictor for dropping out of school.[4]

Research in Chicago indicates that most students at risk of being held back based on a standardized test score are initially motivated to attend summer school to increase their test scores. However, this finding does not hold true for the lowest-scoring students. And, even for those able to raise their test scores, a year later they continue to perform poorly.[5]

In general, students who do not pass a grade the first time around are unlikely to do much better the second time around, all else being equal (which it usually is). So unless cutoff scores are lowered, students will begin to pile up in the lower grades. Worse yet, for those students who repeat a grade twice, chances of dropping out of school soar.[6]

But the real problem is that low-performing students do not benefit either from being passed to the next grade or from being retained in their current grade. For many low-performing students—but not the lowest-performing—summer school focused on test preparation can indeed raise scores in the short run. But no research demonstrates that this immediate payoff has any lasting effect. Whether or not they are retained, these students continue to perform poorly on schoolwork and tests. Thus, it comes as no surprise that students who have been held back in elementary school, particularly the middle grades, have lower rates of going on to higher education than promoted students.[7]

Ending social promotion freezes the already rigid time frame built into the traditional age-graded system for low-performing students.

The Solution, in Our View

Reformers who introduced the idea of standards-based reform talked about the fact that most students could reach the bar, but some would take more time than others. They anticipated that linking high standards to an age-graded system would snare low-performing students. In some cases that has happened.

But the solution to so-called social promotion is neither to pass students to the next grade if they are unprepared nor to hold them back for more of the same. Besides making sure students are as prepared as possible when they begin school, the answer lies in making careful judgments of whether individual students are ready to move to the next level. This, in turn, means figuring out ways to break out of the straitjacket of age-graded schooling that requires everyone to progress at the same rate. Several approaches are possible, each with significant drawbacks. All are needed if low-performing students are to have real chances to succeed.

One approach is to reorganize students by skill level for each subject and move them ahead as they master skills. This results in ungraded classes—that is, classes with students of mixed ages. Nine-year-old Lester might find himself with a group of nine- to eleven-year-olds for math, and he might be grouped with younger students for reading, not his best subject. The drawback is resistance from parents and teachers accustomed to an age-graded school.

Another approach is to identify students with academic problems earlier and to intervene through tutoring and extra instructional time after school, on Saturdays, and during the summer. The challenge lies in hiring and training more teachers and encouraging parents to see that their children attend.

Yet another partial solution is to provide more and better instruction during the regular school day to students at risk of failure. Here the drawback is that the lowest-performing students are unlikely to be assigned the best teachers. And time during the school day for extra instruction is limited.

No single solution will solve all the dilemmas posed by students who fall behind their peers. But for most students, emphasizing prevention of failure in the first place and then providing early intervention and second chances through extra study time are fundamental. As standards are raised, the quality and prevalence of early intervention and second chances need to increase. Simply holding students back—or passing them after intensive test preparation—is not a solution. More time, more supports, and better instruction are.

9

To Track or Not to Track

A T COLUMBIA HIGH School in Maplewood, New Jersey, most of the students are black, although in advanced classes white students make up the vast majority. In the lower math classes, blacks significantly outnumber whites. As one senior put it, "You can tell right away, just by looking into a classroom, what level it is." While the high school boasts of its racial diversity, college-style campus, top scholars, great sports teams, and alumni celebrities, racially segregated classes have prompted protests from its black student leaders. Columbia High, like many other high schools with mixed racial and ethnic populations, strives to celebrate cultural diversity and encourage high academic achievement through tracking.[1]

Tracking, or leveling, is the grouping of students by ability or past performance in middle and high school subjects; educators sometimes refer to it as "homogeneous grouping." The theory behind tracking is that creating classes (e.g., AP Biology, basic math) intended to decrease the disparities in students' capacities increases the chances that teachers can provide instruction tailored to different groups. Tracking assumes that teachers can be patient with low achievers while at the same time push high achievers. High-performing students benefit by not waiting for others to catch up with them. (As one champion of gifted classes asked, "Do we improve the skills of our Olympic swimmers by asking that they take time to teach non-swimmers how to swim?") And low-performing students benefit by not having to compete against high-achievers.[2]

The argument against tracking is that ability groups for top achievers create academic elites and segregate students by race, social class, and ethnicity, thereby depriving low-performing students of peers they can emulate. Moreover, critics argue that grouping low-performing students in separate classes (particularly if they are mostly minority) signals to teachers to lower their academic expectations and deliver an inferior quality of content and skills. As one white student at Columbia High School in a lower-level, predominantly black math class said about the teacher's low expectations: "It makes you feel like you're in a hole."[3]

Debates over district decisions to launch, cut back, or end tracking have broken out at various times across the country. For example, since the 1970s parents of special needs children have pressed to mainstream their children rather than keep them in separate classrooms. Similarly, parents of minority students who have been refused entry into Advanced Placement or honors classes have protested. And researchers, too, have questioned the benefits of leveling and tracking practices.

Current reform efforts to provide a rigorous high school curriculum to all students and NCLB's requirement that all students reach proficiency in reading and math by 2014 add pressure to de-track schools, for how else can all parents be assured that their children have access to what they need to succeed? So conflicts over tracking persist.[4]

Where Did the Idea of Tracking Originate?

Even though educators largely accepted tracking as a worthwhile tool throughout the past century, they debated its effectiveness. After the civil rights movement, court cases, and research studies since the 1960s, however, the debate spilled outside the education community. Since the 1970s, many policymakers, parents, teachers, and researchers have raised serious questions about the accuracy of the tests used to place students in groups, particularly for minority and poor children. They have also questioned the quality of teaching and learning delivered in lower-track classes and the overall worth of ability grouping itself. These debates reflected a social fact: American schools are not only about teaching and learning; they are also virtual ladders to good-paying jobs, higher social status, and a better life. For champions of tracking, sorting students by performance offers students a firm grip on one rung of the ladder.

Research documenting the shortcomings of tracking in secondary schools gained widespread support in the late 1980s. Researchers found that higher percentages of low-income minorities were assigned to lower-level classes than were middle- and upper-middle-income whites. Those lower-level classes were often taught by less-qualified teachers, and the content offered differed from what was taught to upper-level students.

By the early 1990s, the National Governors Association, the National Education Association, the National Council of English Teachers, and the California Department of Education recommended that tracking be abolished. Some districts ended tracking in their middle and high schools.[5] As one researcher said in 1999, "No group of students has been found to benefit consistently from being in a homogenous group."[6]

What Problems Are De-Tracking Intended to Solve?

Sorting students by performance and ability, particularly when that sorting results in large numbers of poor and minority students in low-tracked classes, can amount to a resegregation of students within a school. According to many researchers, policymakers, and practitioners, this segregation is psychologically, educationally, and organizationally harmful to all students in that school. Thus, abolishing tracks in both middle and high schools, and thereby ensuring that all students are in mixed-ability groups, helps students learn from one another in more democratic settings.

Does De-Tracking Work?

Before answering the question of whether de-tracking works, it is important to determine to what degree tracking has been abolished. In

Massachusetts and California, state officials have mandated de-track-ing in middle schools. Districts from across the country have joined the reform as reported by researchers and school boards. Yet, in 1993 researchers found that 86 percent of high schools offered courses in which students were grouped by ability or past performance (90 per-cent in math and 72 percent in English). Of all the public schools in Maryland in 2000, 67 percent reported that they used tracking in four academic subjects. So, while the reform of de-tracking has occurred in some places, tracking remains the dominant practice of organizing instruction in many secondary schools.[7]

What does the research say about de-tracking? Some studies tout the many benefits that flow from mixing students together both for the gifted and lowest-performing students. Students who ordinarily would have been excluded from Advanced Placement courses, for example, were allowed to take the subject and did well on exams. Other studies challenge these findings.

At this time, no researcher, policymaker, or public official can prove whether tracking or de-tracking yields better results in raising aca-demic achievement, getting kids into college, or boosting self-esteem for all students, some, or none at all. Most studies, however, do not assess whether social benefits exist from mixing students of different performance levels and cultural backgrounds, especially since the work world that these students will soon enter does not engage in tracking.[8]

The Solution, in Our View

If research does not settle the question of whether de-tracking works for the most able, least able, and disabled, what is the solution for tracking's negative consequences? The standards, testing, and account-ability movement intends for every student—including disabled and non-English-speaking students—to be, in the language of NCLB, "aca-demically proficient" by 2014, and most parents want their sons and daughters to enter college. In the midst of these high expectations for schools, practices that track students in high school subjects (e.g., AP Biology) remain.

One solution is to allow all students to enroll in academically rigorous classes and to provide the extra help some need to succeed. Structured study groups and tutoring have strong track records as effective ways to provide such help. Similarly, gathering students in need of special help or enrichment at certain times and disbanding such groups when the work is completed seems sensible. But excluding highly motivated, lower-performing students from Advanced Placement or International Baccalaureate courses seems unfair. The challenge lies in balancing the values of equity and achievement at Columbia High and thousands of other high schools.

Another solution is to make certain that seventh- and eighth-grade students, their parents, and their counselors fully understand what is required for different college and career paths. Too often students are locked into a track of coursework in eighth grade that guarantees they will not be prepared for college by their senior year. Many students are totally unaware of this fact.

De-tracking has clearly challenged educators' and parents' assumptions that some students can't handle tough academic subjects by showing that they can if given the opportunity and support. The challenge now is to provide students with the options and the help they need to succeed.

10

Creating Small
Urban High Schools

"AMERICA'S HIGH SCHOOLS are obsolete . . . I am terrified for our workforce," Microsoft chairman Bill Gates told the governors and business leaders who assembled in 2005 to create an agenda for improving high schools.[1] At the National Education Summit on High Schools, high schools were cast as the core education problem facing the country, "the front line in the battle for America's future economic prosperity."[2]

Changes in the global and U.S. economies place new pressures on our high schools. Political and business leaders point to U.S. slippage in international rankings of high school and college graduation rates. As jobs are outsourced to countries where labor is cheaper and workers more motivated, the pressure to increase the academic rigor and the graduation rate of high schools has intensified.

The number of students who are leaving school before graduation is on the rise. Having peaked at close to 80 percent in 1969, the overall U.S. high school graduation rate has dropped over the past decade and is now closer to 70 percent.[3] This means that only seven out of ten students who start high school finish, and half of those are not prepared for college-level work. Of the seven who graduate, four continue their education, and only two finish college on time.[4] For students who are black, Hispanic, or poor, the statistics are much worse. According to the Manhattan Institute, only half of black and Hispanic students finish high school, and most of them are not eligible for college admission: only 20 percent of Hispanic students and 23 percent of black students are college-ready, compared with 40 percent of white students.[5] For youths who are not college-bound, the options are dismal. Often, only dumbed-down, dead-end jobs remain, even for those with a high school diploma.

One response to this situation, fueled by substantial investments from the Bill and Melinda Gates Foundation, is to create small, rigorous high schools. The idea is that high schools with fewer than four hundred students, or roughly one hundred per grade level, provide a more personalized and safer environment than the much larger two-thousand-to four-thousand-student high schools in the biggest cities. Reformers believe that small high schools will encourage more students to stay in school and to graduate ready for college. And, they assert, increasing the academic rigor of coursework will produce more graduates ready for college, thereby reducing the number who must enroll in remedial courses.

Beyond depressing statistics, the physical and social conditions of many large urban high schools are dreadful. They are overcrowded, understaffed, and often dangerous places for students and teachers. Fifty years ago James Conant saw small schools as the enemy of a good high school education because they lacked choices and opportunities for students. Today, these large comprehensive high schools have become the enemy.

The push for small and rigorous high schools specifically targets these big-city schools. By small-school standards, many well-off suburbs also have large high schools yet still send most of their students to college. Palo Alto High School in California graduates virtually all of its 1,700 students, and 90 percent go on to college. Even in the big cities, very large, highly selective high schools are also quite successful. Stuyvesant High School in New York City is huge but unusual because it admits students based on test scores. Out of a student body of 3,200, 99 percent graduate and virtually all go on to college. At the other extreme, many small rural high schools struggle to attract enough well-trained teachers to provide a full range of academic classes. Clearly, size alone does not determine results.

Where Did the High School Reform Concept Originate?

Neither small schools nor a more demanding curriculum is new to the world of high school reform. A push for greater academic rigor, especially in math and science, swept the country in the late 1950s and 1960s in the wake of the Soviet Union's launch of Sputnik, spawning many new math and science textbooks and the Advanced Placement Program. Two decades later, the report *A Nation at Risk* generated a similar wave of attention to academic rigor, inspiring increases in course requirements and tests for graduation.

Small high schools have an equally long history as an unconventional alternative for students and teachers, including continuation schools for students who fail to succeed in regular high schools. Often idealistic in their vision, other small alternative schools have persisted, but most do not survive the departure of their founders. In the 1980s, reformers attempted to establish such alternatives on a larger scale. Ted Sizer's Coalition of Essential Schools spawned a number of small high schools and schools-within-schools in which a subset of teachers and students, usually self-selected, form a small school within a larger high school. During that same period, New York's Central Park East High School, under the leadership of Debbie Meier, attracted attention by creating a school in a poor black district that could graduate students prepared for college. Scores of small high schools in New York and other large cities copied the approach of Central Park East.

However, the idea of hundreds of small high schools replacing large ones is recent. The small-schools movement that had already developed strong local roots in big cities like New York, Philadelphia, and Chicago was greatly expanded by the clout of the Gates Foundation, which has already invested several billion dollars in creating and redesigning high schools.

What Problems Are Small, Rigorous
High Schools Intended to Solve?

Creating small, demanding high schools is aimed at beefing up the supply of college-ready graduates. This means raising both the graduation rate (lowering the dropout rate) and student knowledge so that graduates are prepared for college courses. By replacing large urban high schools with small schools, and by increasing the courses required for graduation, governors and philanthropists hope ultimately to provide the college-educated workforce that American companies need.

Specifically, creating small high schools is expected to overcome the alienation and poor education pervasive in almost all large urban high schools. With fewer students, teachers can get to know each one. Sixteen-year-old George is much more likely to pay attention to a teacher who recognizes him and even knows something about his life outside of school than to a teacher who does not even know his name. In a small school community, teachers can also work together to create a tougher curriculum that is more connected to the world and the lives of their students. As a result, students will be motivated to work harder, learn more, and go to college.

Do Smaller Schools and More
Rigorous Courses Work?

Small schools and more academic rigor do not necessarily go together. One can easily imagine a small school with a weak academic program and a large selective school with a strong one, such as New York City's Stuyvesant.

First, does size matter? In a word, yes—but only in some areas and for some types of small schools. Studies such as the Bank Street College of Education study of Chicago's small schools document some benefits of smallness, including reduced rates of dropouts and course failures and higher grades.[6] Research also suggests that small schools often provide more varied teaching strategies, a safer environment, and more teacher knowledge about individual students. Some studies have documented increases in test scores, but these are not consistent across all types of small schools and tend to show up more in reading than in math. The third-year report of an evaluation of the Gates Foundation's small-schools initiative finds strengths in terms of a positive learning climate for students and attendance but notes a lack of rigor in curriculum and instruction: "we concluded that the quality of student work in all of the schools we studied is alarmingly low."[7]

The benefits of small high schools are usually found in those programs that either operate independently or as a school-within-a-school—that is, those schools chosen by their students and teachers. Moreover, the school-within-a-school approach is effective only when successfully implemented as an autonomous unit.[8] Breaking up a large regular high school into small subunits, known as conversion schools, does not produce the same results and often replaces choice with coercion, particularly for teachers.[9]

What does it take to create rigorous and effective small high schools? New York City has become a laboratory for this very question. In 2003, the chancellor announced a plan to close more than twenty large failing high schools. To replace them, he invited external organizations to create small high schools characterized by rigor, personalization, and community partnerships. By 2007–2008, eighteen nonprofit organizations, with substantial support from the Gates Foundation, had created 123 nonselective small high schools of choice in disadvantaged neighborhoods.[10] Over a few short years, brand new schools serving a few hundred replaced high schools serving thousands of students.

Studies of these new small high schools in New York City find that they emphasize sustained relationships between teachers and students, vary widely in their implementation, and have teachers who tend to be less experienced than their counterparts at larger high schools.[11] New evidence from a rigorous evaluation suggests that students are more likely to graduate from these smaller high schools of choice. For example, 10 percent more are on track to graduate in their freshman year, and graduation rates for one cohort increased almost 7 percent over comparable students attending other schools.[12] No data on academic outcomes beyond progress toward graduation is available. Research on Chicago's two dozen small high schools, also created with major support from the Gates Foundation, found that those with higher levels of student achievement were strong in three areas: teacher professional communities, principal leadership, and teacher influence.[13]

Evidence that large urban high schools do not work for the vast majority of students is quite clear. Particularly discouraging is evidence on the negative impact of increasing academic rigor. When graduation requirements in regular high schools are made more stringent, the dropout rate increases.[14] Graduation rates declined during the same period that course-taking requirements increased. Corroboration comes from interviews with students who say math was the final straw.[15] Promoted without ever understanding the subject matter, they just gave up in algebra or geometry. And those who dropped out were more likely to be minority and poor students.

Dropout rates aside, the increases in course requirements for those who stayed in school had no discernable effect on achievement. Researchers are baffled by the fact that sizable increases in the proportion of students taking a college prep course sequence have not resulted in rising achievement levels on national tests.[16] One likely explanation is the quality of teaching and support for students. Making courses more difficult without ensuring strong teaching would explain this finding. High schools are already hard-pressed to find enough good school leaders and teachers, especially in math and science. And counselors are a disappearing species.

The solution offered by the governors and business leaders—that all students should be required to take algebra 2—seems unlikely to produce the desired results. Just because many adults with the highest-paying jobs took algebra 2 does not mean everyone who takes it will end up with such a job. (Just because all dogs have four legs doesn't mean all animals with four legs are dogs.) The key to increased academic rigor is not the number or names of courses; it is ensuring that the courses are relevant and taught well and that a student has the necessary educational background to learn from them.

Students cannot succeed in any high school course or in the workforce if they cannot read. According to NAEP reading scores in 2003, 38 percent of students about to enter high school (eighth graders) are "below basic." This means they might be able to decipher words—read a page aloud—but they cannot understand what they have read. Adding more rigorous courses to the high school curriculum does not speak to this issue. Schools need the resources to provide intensive interventions in reading, starting well before high school.

The Solution, in Our View

Smaller, more personalized environments make a lot of sense, especially because many teenagers' lack of motivation and misbehavior stand in the way of learning, going to college, and getting a job. It is indeed encouraging that recent evidence finds that the new small high schools of choice in New York increase the likelihood that students will graduate. However, these schools rely heavily on the Gates Foundation for creating a range of alternatives for students whose schools were closed. Overall, the track record of small schools and the challenges to their creation on a large scale argue for pursuing multiple pathways and goals, both for students who drop out and those who graduate.

Rigor has to mean more than "difficult." A rigorous course gets students thinking and working hard—it's not designed simply to weed out those who are not college material. Such courses require teachers and materials that connect to youths and their world. Linking students to the community and to the workplace through projects, service work, and paid work should all be options in the high school curriculum.

"Every kid can graduate ready for college" is an inspiring goal that needs to be bolstered by alternatives for the hundreds of thousands of students who do not make it. That almost two-thirds of minority students admitted to college fail to get a degree within six years speaks to more than high school preparation.[17] Moreover, the public schools are not responsible for the scarcity of productive jobs for anyone without at least a couple of years of college or for the decreasing numbers of slots in many institutions of higher education. The California State University system denied admission to twelve thousand students in 2002–2003 because of cuts in funding, in spite of an increase in high school graduates that year.[18] Eight years later they reduced enrollment by an additional forty thousand students.[19] In many fields, even college graduates have to deal with the economic reality that companies out-source jobs for a host of reasons that are not related to educational background—cost and motivation being paramount.

As a country that prides itself on providing second chances, the United States needs to create more options for the increasing number of young people who leave school early or who are unprepared for a productive future.

11

Turnaround Schools

CONTINENTAL AIRLINES WENT from being ranked worst to best in the airline industry in five years.[1] If failing businesses can manage dramatic turnarounds, why not schools?

Growing desperate over waves of unsuccessful efforts to reform the worst schools in the nation, policymakers seek dramatic cures—from shutting them down to handing them over to charter school operators. "States and districts need to step up and have the political courage to close failing schools and let others try," proclaimed U.S. Secretary of Education Arne Duncan announcing a $4 billion federal investment to turn around the five thousand worst-performing schools in the country.[2]

Previous attempts to transform the lowest-performing schools have been disappointing, especially where essential ingredients for change like leadership and trust are rare commodities. Turnaround strategies aim to wipe the slate clean, one way or another, and build from the ground up, usually with new leadership and increasingly with new staff. Rather than change the entire system of schooling in a district, state, or nation, the goal is to revive or eradicate dreadful schools one at a time. One national magazine dubbed it "Extreme Makeover: School Edition."[3]

Where Did the Idea of
Turnaround Schools Originate?

Education reformers appropriated the "turnaround" lingo from the business world, where strategies like Total Quality Management have been around for decades. In fact, much of what we know about turning around organizations comes from studies of corporate turnarounds. The idea is dramatic change quickly. "Right Away and All at Once" is the title of the story of the Continental Airlines turnaround.

Applying the idea of turnaround to schools has seeds in the effective schools and school improvement movements of the 1970s and 1980s that was grounded in the belief that schools with mostly poor and minority students do not have to be unsafe and low performing. Under the right conditions, a hopeless school can become safe, well organized, and high performing. Then, as now, however, it's much easier to identify the correlates of school effectiveness than it is to put them in place where they're missing.

In the early 1980s, San Francisco became the testing ground for a new remedy for low achievement called *reconstitution*. Mandated by a federal court decree to racially integrate the schools, all the staff in low-performing segregated schools were to be forcibly transferred with an option to apply to return under new leadership.[4] Students also had to reapply. Although the first round of four reconstituted schools led to higher test scores, the conditions—extra money, reduced class sizes, and parent choice and commitment—could not be replicated in later rounds. The strategy was put on hold for a decade until a commission overseeing desegregation reinvigorated the process, leading to ten reconstituted schools.

In the 1990s, with the entry of standards-based reform, the federal government sponsored the development of models of whole-school reform intended to provide blueprints for schools needing to raise student achievement. With the advent of No Child Left Behind, test score accountability became the driving force, and schools that failed to make adequate yearly progress were labeled "in need of improvement" officially, or, more commonly, "failing." NCLB raised the stakes on fixing schools that repeatedly failed to make adequate progress according to the law. By their fifth year of "needing improvement," schools must restructure using one of five options prescribed in the law, including replacing school staff or contracting with an outside agency to run the school. Most, however, chose the "major restructuring" option that provided few specifics beyond producing "fundamental reform."

These options morphed into a narrower set of options proposed by the Obama administration in 2010 for schools wanting a School Turnaround Grant: fire the principal and at least half the staff, reopen as a charter, or close the school and transfer students to better schools in the district—in other words, rapid and dramatic change.

What Problems Are Turnaround Schools Intended to Solve?

Fundamentally, the turnaround schools strategy is to increase achievement rapidly in chronically low-performing schools. The goal is to clear the public school system of the worst schools, those that consistently produce the lowest test score gains and highest dropout rates. The perennial problem is how to accomplish this Herculean task. Here the turnaround strategy takes on two problems: how to get rid of weak principals and teachers and how to fundamentally and quickly inspire and support teachers sufficiently to engage children in learning and achieving.

Do Turnaround Schools Work?

There's little evidence that turnaround strategies will fare much better than previous efforts to improve low-performing schools. In fact, there's little evidence on turnaround strategies at all. The U.S. Department of Education says as much in their purportedly evidence-based guide for turning schools around, which is, at best, underwhelming in available studies.[5]

More research does exist for turnarounds in the private sector or business world, but these studies do not encourage optimism. About a quarter of businesses that launched turnaround initiatives ended up with new management techniques and organizational improvement, but they did not show evidence of increased economic performance.[6] Much of the history of school reform efforts paints a similar picture. There is some evidence of organizational changes in a minority of cases, but it's not lasting and doesn't offer much that affects the bottom line in schooling: graduation and dropout rates and test scores.

One reason for limited research is that strategies to reconstitute or close failing schools have not been widespread. But the handful of studies that exist reach similar conclusions: replacing teachers provides no guarantee of improvement in the schools' quality. San Francisco, Chicago, and Portland, among others, all have stories of reconstituted high schools that resulted in staffs of substitutes and new teachers without experience or credentials and with only few veterans to rely on. A study of reconstituted schools found little impact on staff quality, school organization, or school performance.[7] Even the U.S. Department of Education's own guide, "Turning Around Chronically Low-Performing Schools," states that "the school turnaround case studies and the business turnaround research do not support the wholesale replacement of staff." The exceptions are cases like the first wave of reconstituted schools in San Francisco, in which extra elements—including resources and parent involvement—were key. But in districts already struggling to find enough qualified staff, reconstitution does not appear to be an effective strategy. It can also have unintended consequences—human costs to respected and effective teachers who are suddenly without a teaching position and who are treated as pariahs by other schools.

Permanently closing failing schools is only workable when schools are not already filled to capacity and have a higher reputation for academic achievement than the closed school. Meeting these conditions is challenging in urban districts and impossible in rural districts. Success of the strategy can be seen by how well students perform in their new schools. Chicago researchers tracked students from closed schools and found that most reenrolled in academically weak schools and, except for the few attending high scoring schools, were no better off academically one year later.[8]

Another variant of the turnaround strategy—takeover by a charter organization or other outside agency—has a mixed track record. Like traditional public schools, some charters are effective and many are not. Philadelphia's experience with outsourcing the management of forty-five schools found that even with additional expenditures, increases in student achievement were no greater in those managed by outside organizations than those remaining under district management.[9] Some charter groups have shown short-term success but have done so by expanding slowly and do not have the ability to expand quickly without watering down their approach.[10]

Studies of organizations that have successfully turned schools around are characterized first and foremost by strong leaders who diagnose the particulars of the schools they lead. They may be fired-up veteran principals or a new breed of turnaround specialists. But their numbers are limited and their schools usually regress when they leave—and that's in the cases when they are effective in the first place. At the end of 2007, the state of Maryland, frustrated with the lack of results from interventions in persistently low-performing schools, decided to abandon the strategy of turnaround specialists.[11]

Findings from case studies of schools in six states required to restructure under NCLB also found that replacing school staff or contracting with an outside organization did not show promise. Schools that improved used multiple, coordinated strategies tailored to their particular circumstances and then continually revised them.[12]

The long-term work of the Consortium on Chicago School Reform underscores these lessons. Based on fifteen years of data, researchers identified five keys to students' achievement gains: strong and inclusive leadership, links to parents and the community, development of teacher's professional capacity, a safe and stimulating learning climate, plus strong instructional guidance and materials.[13] Although more detailed, these elements are similar to those historically associated with effective schools. But this study uncovered more. These elements are far more effective in tandem than they are alone, and they are unlikely to be found in the worst schools—schools in neighborhoods characterized by public housing and high rates of crime, child abuse and neglect, and homelessness. Remedies for these most troubled schools are unlikely to work unless such schools can form alliances with community organizations to tackle out-of-school problems.

THE COMMUNITY ROLE IN TURNAROUND SCHOOLS

Few models for turning around schools take seriously the role of the community in spite of growing evidence of its importance. Two that have done so are the School Development Project and the Harlem Children's Zone. Both exhibit evidence of effectiveness, according to federal studies.

The School Development Project, designed by psychiatrist James Comer at Yale University in 1969, rests on the theory that children's poor academic performance is in large part due to the school's failure to bridge the social, psychological, and cultural gaps between home and school. Turning around a school academically depends on creating a climate in the school where a community of adults—the principal, parents, teachers, community leaders, health-care workers—and children can develop work smoothly together to improve academic achievement. The approach emphasizes problem solving by consensus and without blame.

Comer schools create governance structures that support collaborative problem solving, including a School Planning and Management Team comprised of school staff, parents, and a child development specialist; a Mental Health Team made up of school staff together with psychologists, social workers, and nurses; and a Parents' Group that aims at involving parents in all aspects of the school. It is supported primarily by public funds in districts that adopt the program.

The Harlem Child's Zone, started in the late 1990s by Geoffrey Canada, aims to rebuild a community by intervening in children's lives as early as possible and building a critical mass of adults who understand what it takes to help children succeed. It includes a charter

The Solution, in Our View

Walking through the halls of the worst-performing schools in the country, it is not hard to understand the desire of policymakers to shut them down. Signs of teaching are few and far between, with teachers struggling for control and students wandering the halls. Yet, reform history elementary and middle school—Promise Academies—and surrounds them with almost two dozen programs, including a nine-week parenting workshop for expectant parents and those with young children, an asthma initiative that provides education and medical care to families, and a network of afterschool programs. The program also operates a health clinic in the middle school. These services are supported primarily by wealthy individuals and private foundations.

Repeated scrutiny of Comer schools by researchers and independent evaluators has determined that, when the design is fully implemented, the programs have moderate to strong effects on student achievement in largely minority and poor elementary schools. The Promise Academies are much newer so have had less scrutiny. However, one rigorous study concluded that the Promise Academy middle school appears to increase students' math scores significantly.

SOURCES

Comer School. http://info.med.yale.edu/comer/about_comer.html.

Cook, Thomas D., Robert F. Murphy, and H. David Hunt. "Comer's School Development Program in Chicago: A Theory-Based Evaluation." *American Educational Research Journal* 37, no. 2 (2000): 535–597. http://www.northwestern.edu/ipr/publications/comer.pdf .

Harlem Children's Zone. http://www.hcz.org/.

Robbie, Will, and Roland G. Fryer Jr. *Are High Quality Schools Enough to Close the Achievement Gap? Evidence from a Social Experiment in Harlem.* NBER Working Paper No. 15473. Cambridge, MA: National Bureau of Economic Research, 2009.

is clear: permanently closing the schools or replacing the adults in the school without substantial investments in parallel changes is bound to disappoint.

Radical turnaround strategies, whether restaffing public schools or expanding charter schools, require a large pool of qualified and motivated teachers and an energetic, astute leader. Without investing in that kind of leader and the development of such a pool—whether current or prospective teachers—radical surgery holds little promise. It's a short-sighted strategy for unloading weak teachers.

Imagining speeded-up reform in the most challenging schools flies in the face of all that we know. A serious approach to the lowest-performing schools across the country would acknowledge each school's context and the realities it faces. It would make a long-term commitment to building the school's leadership. A realistic approach would have many of the same components recommended by turnaround specialists: careful diagnosis in determining the starting place with the most promise and building the skills and knowledge of those responsible for student learning. It would also seriously engage teachers and the community from the beginning in setting goals and putting them into practice. Replacing staff or redefining roles may be necessary, but starting with a presumption that communicates contempt for the practitioners who are responsible for carrying out the work will undermine what follows.[14] Above all, those leading change must be committed to the long haul and have the conviction and adequate support to do so.

12

Reducing Class Size

WOULD YOU WANT your first grader in a class of fifteen students or thirty students? Would you rather teach twenty students or thirty students? The notion of fewer students per class carries tremendous gut appeal for parents and teachers alike. Few strategies for improving achievement are embraced as enthusiastically as reducing class size. Students receive more individual attention. Teachers can spend more time teaching instead of managing and disciplining. Struggling students are less likely to fall through the cracks.

However—and it's a big however—reducing class size is among the most expensive reform strategies because it requires more of the most costly resources in education: teachers and classroom space. Do its benefits justify such major expenses? Do students actually learn more in smaller classes?

Where Did the Idea Originate?

In the late nineteenth century, classes in big cities had between fifty and seventy-five students. In the early twentieth century, education progressives introduced the idea of focusing on the individual child, which drew attention to reducing class sizes. These days, class sizes range from fifteen to forty students, depending on the locale and the grade level.[1]

Today, reducing class sizes appeals intuitively to parents and teachers: the fewer students in a classroom, the more attention each will get, and more individual attention will lead to more learning. From the teacher's perspective, small classes are easier to manage. From the parent's perspective, the child is less likely to get lost and fall behind.

Support for small classes is strongest in the earliest grades. Results from a well-publicized study of K–3 class size in Tennessee in the 1980s have been taken as proof that students learn more in smaller classes. The study found that students do learn more when classes have fewer than seventeen students. In fact, minority students gained more than majority students in the first two years of the study and maintained that edge for the second two years.[2] And the advantage persisted years later.[3] Because the Tennessee study is one of the few randomized experiments to take place in education research, its results are viewed by many as conclusive evidence that small class size can increase both achievement and equity.

What Problem Is Reducing Class Size Intended to Solve?

Large classes pose myriad problems for teachers, parents, and students. Smaller classes do not guarantee more individual attention, but they are, at the very least, a necessary condition for it. From grading student work to organizing classroom activities, more students also usually means more work for the teacher. Organizing students in groups, engaging students in projects, providing different activities for different students—all these activities are more difficult with larger class sizes.

Although most class size reduction debates and policies focus on the early grades, middle grade and high school teachers must also limit the amount of work they assign. Imagine a typical high school English teacher with five classes of thirty-five students each. Grading a four-page essay means carefully reading and marking seven hundred pages of work. Even at a good clip—say thirty seconds per page—this translates into six hours of work. A more reasonable minute-per-page pace is close to twelve hours. No wonder such assignments are rare.

The more students, the more discipline problems, and the more a teacher's time is spent on classroom management instead of teaching. The more students, the less likely a teacher will notice when a particular student gets stuck and the less likely that a teacher will be able to answer every pupil's questions.

Does Reducing Class Sizes Work?

Yes and no. Smaller classes, especially in the early grades, can make a big difference, but only if they are quite small. Studies of class size, including the Tennessee study, demonstrate higher achievement when classes contain seventeen or fewer students for several years in a row. The Tennessee study suggests that the benefits make their biggest impact in the first two grades and that the effect lasts throughout a child's school years. The effects were the greatest for minority students in the first two years of school. This is the time when students need to learn, in addition to academic content, a variety of new behaviors and social skills to function in a school setting.[4]

However, states and districts typically can afford only to shrink classes in the first few grades of elementary school a little bit—from thirty to twenty-eight or even as low as twenty, as California did in 1996 (but has recently backed off in response to the state fiscal crisis.) But few, if any, places can afford to guarantee classes with fewer than twenty students.

When classes have twenty or more students, the evidence of improved learning is not convincing. One reason may be that not enough teachers know how to teach in ways that take advantage of small classes. Another explanation is that the quality of the teaching generally matters more than the number of students. Students are usually better off in a class with thirty students and really good teaching than in a class with twenty students and poor teaching.

Sudden shifts to smaller class sizes also cause unexpected problems. California's statewide class size reduction law, passed in 1996, had the effect of increasing the gap between poor and rich districts. Reducing class size to twenty children in kindergarten through third grade in every school in the state meant that every school had to hire new teachers and find additional classroom space—a boon to the portable classroom industry. This dramatic increase in demand for more teachers resulted in districts hiring many teachers without credentials. Most of these uncredentialed teachers ended up in schools serving the most disadvantaged students.[5]

The Solution, in Our View

Given the huge expense of reducing class size, it is not a realistic option for most school systems. However, several solutions are worth considering. One is to reduce class size only in schools with students who will benefit the most: schools with predominantly poor and minority students. Within these schools, the first priority should be the primary grades. In fact, Tennessee put the findings of class-size research into practice in just this way. The state funded smaller kindergarten through third-grade classes in sixteen of the state's poorest districts. These districts improved their statewide ranking, rising from the bottom to near the middle.[6]

Another solution would be to organize students in smaller and larger groups depending on the learning activity. Masterful teachers organize classes into groups, some of which require minimal teacher involvement, freeing the teacher to work intensively with a small group. In fact, some student activities can be done in quite large groups, enabling teachers to work with a few struggling students. The risk is that students working without direct teacher involvement will benefit less. Some schools, elementary and secondary, manage to schedule time during the day when students can all work with teachers in small groups of ten to twelve by using all regular and specialist teachers.

Ultimately, the greater the emphasis on helping teachers teach better and on providing teachers with help in handling disruptive students, the less class size will matter. Students are better off in a large class with good teaching than in a small class with poor teaching. So investing in better teacher preparation and opportunities for current teachers to keep learning should be weighed against the expense of reducing class size.

13

More Time in School

I F STUDENTS LEARN while in school, they will learn more if they
are in school longer. So goes the logic. Extending students' time in
school makes sense to reformers and policymakers. They assume
that adding hours to the school day and days to the school year will
result in higher test scores. Moreover, to reduce the test score achievement gap between minority and white students, reformers promote an
extended school day and summer school to give an extra boost to students who need to catch up.

Although these reforms are expensive, research studies have found
that students who spend more time on learning tasks also score higher
on tests. Fortifying the case for more time in school are test results
from nearly fifty countries that show the amount of instructional time
spent on math and science is linked strongly to achievement scores.[1]

Just how much time do American students spend in school? Typically, more than fifty million students go to public school from five to
six hours a day 180 days a year. Generally, schools open and close at
about the same time each day across the country. From midafternoon
to dinnertime each day and all day during the summer, working parents—now the majority of moms and dads—have to scramble to find
adult supervision for their children.

When summers and other vacations are added up, children and youth spend 80 percent of their waking hours *out of school*. Surveys find that on a daily basis, they watch TV and play video games more than they sit in classrooms. All of that time out of school, much of it unsupervised for large numbers of children, does not make sense to most policymakers and many parents. They see other nations that require more time in school than the United States performing better on international tests. As the National Education Commission on Time and Learning concluded in 1994, the "uniform six-hour day and a 180-day year is the unacknowledged design flaw in American education."[2]

So reform proposals for year-round schools, afterschool programs, extended school days, and a longer school year find welcoming audiences among both policymakers and parents.

Where Did the Idea of Increasing Time in School Originate?

The traditional nine-month school calendar with a summer break comes from the nineteenth-century agrarian origins of tax-supported public schools. Farm families needed extra hands to help out at critical times of the year. As the United States became industrialized and urbanized, challenges to a farm-based school calendar arose prior to and after World War II, but especially in the last quarter-century as major societal changes arose. These included changes in family composition when many more mothers entered the labor market full time and heightened criticism of public schools as American students recorded lackluster performances on international tests. Yet the traditional calendar persists.

Most efforts to increase the amount of instructional time have taken the form of longer days, a longer school year, summer school, or year-round schools, which actually change the structure of the school calendar.

In 1988, 13 percent of all public schools offered extended-day programs such as afterschool centers; a decade later, 63 percent did so. Many charter and for-profit schools offer more time in school than do regular public schools. Knowledge Is Power Program (KIPP) schools across the country, for example, start school at 7:30 a.m. and close at 5 p.m. on weekdays and are open four hours on Saturday and a month during the summer. As of 2010, the Center for American Progress identified 655 schools in thirty-six states with extended school days or years, one quarter of which are standard district public schools.[3] Of course, this is only a tiny fraction of the roughly ninety thousand public schools nationwide. The first American year-round school (varied calendar versions exist) opened in 1976. Today, there are just over three thousand year-round public schools (less than 4 percent of total schools) in forty-six states (most located in California) with two-thirds of these being elementary schools.[4]

Under pressure to increase test scores and close the achievement gap, educators have imposed limits on nonacademic activities during the day to increase the amount of instructional time. As the Atlanta superintendent of schools who got rid of recess in elementary schools in 1998 put it, "We are intent on improving academic performance. You don't do that by having kids hanging on the monkey bars."[5]

What Problem Is Spending More Time in School Intended to Solve?

More time in school offers solutions to a host of problems that result from the expanding global economy and consequent pressures to increase test scores. NCLB also puts pressure on schools to increase test scores for all students. Increasing instructional time, by adding time or subtracting nonacademic activities, could be one solution.

Closing the achievement gap ups the ante. The lowest-performing students must increase their rate of learning for the gap to close. Reformers propose more instructional time for the lowest-performing students as a way of boosting their achievement. Some research suggests that low-income students forget more over the summer than their counterparts who have more opportunities to learn in their homes, at summer camp, or on vacations. Reformers argue that more learning time for these students in the summer can keep the achievement gap from increasing during these months.[6] In fact, one study finds that it is the summer gap in schooling that accounts for more than half the cumulative gap in test scores between low- and high-poverty students by ninth grade.[7] And with more parents working to maintain their standard of living, more time in school is also a way of easing the intense pressure of finding satisfactory child care.

Does More Time in School Work?

Researchers have tried to show a link between more time spent in school and test score improvement. It is tough for researchers to disentangle the payoff in test score gains of increasing the time spent in school (or after school) from other innovations that usually accompany changing school schedules. New texts, new technologies, professional development of teachers, changing school populations, turnover in teachers and principals all factor into the year-to-year mix of test score gain, stability, or loss. So the benefits have been hard to prove—except for one point.

Evidence from many studies demonstrates that simply adding hours to the day, days to the year, reducing recess, or launching a new afterschool program does not in itself yield improved academic achievement. What matters is how that time is spent in the classroom. Adding five or ten days to the school calendar, switching to a year-round calendar, or extending the school day does not necessarily translate to students focusing on academic tasks. What counts is the actual time students spend learning subject matter and skills.

The effects of more time are cumulative. Even a high-quality summer program for low-performing students cannot substitute for effective instruction during the school year. Students who benefited from Chicago's Summer Bridge program returned to their low performance the following school year.[8] However, attending summer school for several years in a row can have a significant impact. Based on a rigorous randomized study in Baltimore, researchers found that students from high-poverty schools who attended summer school for two or three years gained almost half an entire grade level relative to the control group that did not.[9]

The Solution, in Our View

If more time in school is spent doing just more of the same, the goal of increased achievement will not be realized. In converting more time in school into classroom academic gains, the teacher is the gatekeeper. Longer school days, afterschool programs, and summer programs can increase student achievement only if teachers succeed in motivating attendance and in providing high-quality instruction. Thus, efforts aimed at strengthening teaching are critical.[10]

To the extent that options for additional time are voluntary, as is true with many afterschool and summer programs, those who need it the most may not attend. So another part of the solution is making extra effort to provide the help and support families need to be sure their children attend.

Although strong evidence for increased gains in test scores is missing, extending the day and adding days to the school calendar can be justified on grounds of cost if teachers fully participate in making the additional time academically worthwhile with better-prepared lessons and a more engaging curriculum. Additional time in school also can be justified on other grounds: the relief it can bring to parents knowing that their children are safe in settings where staff care for their well-being and can provide educationally enriching experiences.

Ultimately, it's worth considering paying teachers for twelve months rather than nine thereby increasing the likelihood that summer school programs are staffed with experienced practitioners. Twelve-month contracts also mean that teachers have more time to prepare classroom materials, upgrade their skills, and work with others to improve instruction. Unfortunately, when recessions occur, shrinking education budgets often lead to the opposite: shorter school years and canceled summer school programs for those who need it most.

14

Scaling Up Best
Practices

B EST PRACTICES EXIST in every field, from corporate management to NASCAR. In fact, there are thousands, if not hundreds of thousands, of best practices within every profession,
if searches on the Internet are any indication. The idea is simple and
compelling. Some corporations are more profitable than others, some
racetracks are safer than others, some schools score higher than others.
So it makes sense that organizations that are not doing as well might
look to others and ask, What are you doing to get better results?

The desire to learn from others has produced a raft of studies of best
practices in education. From the "unusually effective" schools of the
1970s to the "beating the odds" schools of the early 2000s, these studies identify schools with poor and minority students that perform better
than expected and seek to identify the practices that led to these results.

Today's best practices, deduced from observations of schools with
increasing test scores and decreasing achievement gaps, fill the crav-
ing for specific suggestions to improve test scores that accountability
pressures have generated. Popularly dubbed "research-based," few are
actually based on rigorous research, and those that are merely establish
effectiveness or lack thereof in the cases studied.

For a school or district looking to improve, the challenge is to figure out what conditions in the best practice site enabled a practice to flourish and whether the struggling site has those conditions. Are the students similar? Is it the practices themselves or the skills of the people using them that makes the difference in student achievement? How much teacher professional development was available? What other pieces have to be in place?

Here's an example. A best practice that appears on several such lists is frequent monitoring of student performance. In schools where this is done well, many other elements are in place. A successful school that monitors student performance well is likely to be in a district that has created useful assessments to measure progress, provided extensive training to teachers, scheduled time for teachers to discuss results, and established an easy-to-use data system so that teachers can enter and retrieve data on individual students as needed. If a school simply adopts a new test for monitoring students without the other pieces, it will likely fail to produce the desired results. Even with all these pieces in place, the question remains of whether teachers have the knowledge to act on what they learn from the assessments.

Under time pressure to improve, educators often embrace practices reputed to be best that appear to meet their needs without figuring out whether the necessary conditions are in place.

Where Did the Idea Originate?

In 1966, the federally commissioned Coleman Report made a big splash. Its conclusion—that a student's family background has a bigger impact on academic achievement than school quality—was often taken to mean that schools cannot make a difference. One response was to demonstrate that some schools clearly do.

In the early 1970s, a handful of researchers began looking at urban schools where students were performing above national norms. Building on this work, researcher Ronald Edmonds identified additional schools where poor children had higher test scores than expected given their backgrounds. He compiled a list of practices these effective schools had in common and launched a movement to help other schools establish these practices. Edmonds' five factors have been expanded and amended, but the essence of each one remains on almost every list of best practices: strong principal leadership, a pervasive instructional focus, orderly and safe climate, high expectations for students, and continuous assessment of student achievement.[1]

Edmonds and his successors rested their work on the presumption that if some children from poor families can succeed, all can. If some teachers repeatedly produce large achievement gains with poor children, all can. If some schools with mostly poor children repeatedly produce high test scores gains, all can. Although these claims stretch credulity, the underlying motive is compelling: the belief that schools can improve and that poverty and race are not excuses for providing substandard education—hence, the hunt for schools and districts that can serve as proof that it is possible.

The idea of looking at exemplars to figure out what works got a second wind in the 1980s when Tom Peters and other observers of successful corporations spread the lingo of benchmarking and best practices.[2] The standards movement's banner, "all children can learn," and the requirement of the federal No Child Left Behind Act that all subgroups of students meet certain test score targets each year added motivation to find practices that yield gains. As attention has shifted in recent years to the role of the school district, best practices research has turned attention to what districts do as well as individual schools.

Study after study has generated descriptions of practices found in schools with unusually high test scores. Some provide lists of practices, while others have fuller descriptions and back them up with detailed case studies of individual schools and districts that give a sense of their history and how the practices fit together. Most descriptions of best practices converge on a set of factors not unlike those originally identified by Edmonds. Although the broad brush strokes remain the same, the specific practices shift over time as reform trends change in emphasis. In the early 1980s, for example, one best practice for districts, called school-based management, was to delegate decisions about curriculum and other matters to individual schools. Today, it is a best practice for districts to use a single districtwide curriculum for all schools.

Although best practices seem to go hand in hand with high test scores, the research provides no guarantee that the practices themselves cause higher scores—hence, the importance of understanding the broader set of conditions that contribute to higher scores.

What Problem Is Best
Practices Intended to Solve?

The idea behind identifying the practices of successful schools and districts is that others who are less successful can learn how to improve. But the problems that need solving are not simple ones.

Districts and schools do not purposely choose ineffective practices. Most aim to do well by their students. So why are some less successful than others? Perhaps the real problem lies in understanding the answer to this question—that is, what are we doing wrong here? Different answers may suggest different courses of action.

Some best practices are self-evident. Kati Haycock of the Education Trust points to funding gaps between districts with the most and the fewest poor children as well as to gaps in the quality of teachers and curriculum between the poorest and the least-poor students.[3] Here the problem is not one of ignorance about what would help close the achievement gap; the problem is how to reduce gaps in funding and teacher and curriculum quality.

Other kinds of problems are more amenable to best practices research. Say a school or district has just adopted a new reading program. If a similar district adopted the same program a few years earlier and found it effective, what steps did it take? For example, what kind of training did teachers get, what problems did they encounter, how did they solve them? In short, how did they create the conditions for the best practice to work?

Do Best Practices Work?

Well-documented practices from similar schools that have performed well year after year can provide a starting point for educators working to improve their schools. Reading about, and especially talking to, those involved at successful sites can be both inspiring and open the door to new ways of thinking and new strategies. But the limitations need to be clear from the outset in order to avoid false promises.

Best practices are not magic bullets. Some success stories rely on exceptional people or circumstances, such as a school whose teachers and students have chosen to be there. What works in these circumstances is unlikely to work elsewhere. Other best practices are a flash in the pan, successful only for a brief time—or perhaps for a somewhat longer sizzle. But a change in principal or test or district mandates, or simply the passage of time, changes the results. The high turnover rate of teachers and principals in urban schools makes sustained efforts difficult. Even the excellent companies identified in the best seller *In Search of Excellence* were no longer excellent a few years later. Many went downhill; some even folded.[4]

Studies identifying schools that outperform other schools with similar student bodies leave many questions unanswered. One is whether test scores, especially an average score based on one year, really indicate effectiveness. A school can have high scores in third-grade math and low scores in third-grade reading one year and the reverse a year later. Or high scores in all subjects in one third-grade class and not the other. Or high scores in third grade and low scores in fourth grade. On average, one school might appear to be better than another, but it may only be a few exceptional teachers—or a few exceptional students—who account for this difference. In other cases, the unmeasured characteristics of students (e.g., many are technically poor but only because their parents are graduate students at Harvard) and the presence of unusual circumstances lead to questionable claims of success.[5]

Another unanswered question about best practices is just how they led to higher-than-expected student achievement. Studies typically inquire about best practices and describe what is going on in the schools and districts that produce higher-than-expected test scores, but they are not able to link the practices directly to the results. So, for example, many studies conclude that instructional leadership is a best practice and may go further to describe the specific things an instructional leader does. But this list of behaviors is still many steps removed from what a teacher, principal, or superintendent actually needs to do to raise student test scores.

Practices that work well in one school may not fit in another. Their success inevitably depends on a particular combination of interconnected practices, the skills and knowledge of the people using them, the school's history of innovation, and the conditions likely to support changes in their school. Transplanting practices is akin to transplanting a tree. Unless the soil conditions are appropriate, the tree is unlikely to survive.

Even knowing the whole story behind a successful school does not tell others how to duplicate its winning ways. The essence of good practice is what goes on between a teacher and a student in a particular lesson. Program developers and education reformers would be out of business if this could be boiled down to a set of easy-to-follow steps.

The Solution, in Our View

Models of good practice are critical. They demonstrate what is possible. They suggest what the ingredients of success are. Whether the practices are those of an excellent teacher, an inspired principal, or a district's system for recruiting top educators, those who can observe good practice for an extended time begin to see how all the pieces fit together. But opportunities are rare for extended firsthand observation among education practitioners. Moreover, the distance between observing practice and duplicating it schoolwide, much less across a district, is huge. So it is not surprising that success on a small scale rarely becomes widespread. Most successes depend on too many specific conditions that often remain unidentified or cannot be replicated.

Many of the frameworks developed in the process of documenting successful schools and districts provide useful guides for educators to analyze their own organizations. The more that studies of best practices emphasize how and why certain results occurred, the more useful they will be to educators. The more such studies provide models of how educators can ask good questions about why their school or district is ineffective with some or all students, the more likely it is that educators will figure out solutions that match their schools or districts.

Best practices cannot be easily transplanted, but the process of thinking through the problems they are intended to solve can lead to better solutions. In fact, this process can rightly shift the emphasis from transplanting one or two flowers to improving the soil.

15

Principals as Instructional Leaders

EFFECTIVE MANAGER? Savvy politician? Heroic leader? Reformers press for principals who can not only play these roles but also raise test scores and do so quickly. These days principals can earn thousands of dollars in bonuses for boosting student achievement—as much as $12,000 extra in Prince George's County, Maryland, and Pittsburgh, Pennsylvania, and up to $25,000 in New York City.[1]

Principals are expected to maintain order and be shrewd managers who squeeze a dollar out of every dime spent on the school and astute politicians who can steer parents, teachers, and students in the same direction year after year. They are also expected to ensure that district curriculum standards are being taught as well as to lead instructional improvement that will translate into test score gains.

Being a principal is a tall order. As one New York City small high school principal put it, "You're a teacher, you're Judge Judy, you're a mother, you're a father, you're a pastor, you're a therapist, you're a nurse, you're a social worker." She took a breath and continued. "You're a curriculum planner, you're a data gatherer, you're a budget scheduler, you're a vision spreader." Yet, at the end of the day, the pressures and rewards are for raising test scores and graduation rates, today's measure of instructional leadership.[2]

Where Did the Idea of Instructional Leadership Originate?

Historically, the title *principal* comes from the phrase "principal teacher," a teacher who was designated by a mid-nineteenth-century school board to manage the nonclassroom tasks of schooling a large number of students and turning in reports. Principals examined students personally to see what was learned, evaluated teachers, created curriculum, and took care of the business of schooling. So from the creation of the job more than 150 years ago, principals were expected to play both managerial and instructional roles.[3]

Over the decades, however, district expectations for principals' instructional role have grown without being clarified or without lessening managerial and political responsibilities. Over the past quarter-century, the literature on principals has shifted markedly from managing budgets, maintaining the building, hiring personnel, and staff decision making to being primarily about instruction. And, within the past decade, their being held directly accountable for student results on tests has been added to the instructional role. As instructional leaders, principals now must also pay far closer attention to activities they hope will help teachers produce higher student scores, such as aligning the school curriculum to the state test.[4]

Today's reformers put forth different ideas of what instructional leaders should do to meet standards and increase achievement. Some argue that principals need to know what good instruction looks like, spend time in classrooms, analyze teachers' strengths and weaknesses, and provide helpful feedback. Other reformers say principals need to motivate teachers and provide opportunities for teachers to learn from each other and from professional development.[5] Still others say principals should focus on data, continually analyzing student test scores to pinpoint where teachers need help.

The list goes on. Some reformers argue that principals should exercise instructional leadership by hiring the right curriculum specialists or coaches to work with teachers on improving instruction. Finally, others suggest that the most efficient way to improve instruction and achievement is to get rid of the bad teachers and hire good ones, an option not always open to leaders of struggling schools. Most of these ideas are not mutually exclusively but together pose a Herculean task, one in addition to all the other responsibilities that refuse to simply disappear.

What Problem Is the Principal as Instructional Leader Intended to Solve?

The short answer is raise a school's low academic performance. The mission statement of New Leaders for New Schools, a program that trains principals for urban schools, captures the expectation that principals can end low academic performance through their instructional leadership: "Our leaders are influential agents of change who impact not only students and schools but entire communities, producing high school graduates well prepared for college, careers, and beyond. It is our mission to ensure high academic achievement for every student by attracting and preparing outstanding leaders and supporting the performance of the urban public schools they lead at scale."[6]

Such rhetoric and the sharp focus on the principal as an instructional leader in current policymaker talk have made principals into heroic figures who can turn around failing schools, reduce the persistent achievement gap single-handedly, and leap tall buildings in a single bound.

If the immediate problem is low academic performance, then the practical problem principals must solve is how to influence what teachers do daily, since it is their impact on student learning that will determine gains and losses in academic achievement.

Does Principal Instructional Leadership Work?

The research we reviewed on stable gains in test scores across many different approaches to school improvement all clearly points to the principal as the catalyst for instructional improvement. But being a catalyst does not identify which specific actions influence what teachers do or translate into improvements in teaching and student achievement.

Researchers find that what matters most is the context or climate in which the actions occur. For example, classroom visits, or walk-throughs, are a popular vehicle for principals to observe what teachers are doing. Principals might walk into classrooms with a required check-list designed by the district and check off items, an approach likely to misfire. Or the principal might have a short list of expected classroom practices created or adopted in collaboration with teachers in the con-text of specific school goals for achievement. The latter signals a setting characterized by collaboration and trust within which an action by the principal is more likely to be influential than in a context of mistrust and fear.[7]

So research does not point to specific surefire actions that instruc-tional leaders can take to change teacher behavior and student learn-ing. Instead, what is clear from studies of schools that do improve is that a cluster of factors account for the change.[8]

Over the past forty years, factors associated with raising a school's academic profile include teachers' consistent focus on academic stan-dards and frequent assessment of student learning, a serious school-wide climate of learning, district support, and parental participation.[9] Recent research also points to the importance of mobilizing teach-ers and the community to move in the same direction, building trust among all the players, and especially creating working conditions that support teacher collaboration and professional development.[10]

In short, a principal's instructional leadership combines both direct actions, such as observing and evaluating teachers, and indirect ac-tions, such as creating school conditions that foster improvements in teaching and learning.[11] How principals do this varies from school to school—particularly between elementary and secondary schools, given their considerable differences in size, teacher knowledge, daily sched-ules, and students' plans for their future.[12] Yes, keeping their eye on instruction can contribute to stronger instruction and even higher test scores. But close monitoring of instruction can only influence, not en-sure, such improvement.

Moreover, learning to carry out this role as well as all the other duties of the job takes time and experience. Both of these are in short supply, especially in urban districts where principal turnover rates are high.[13]

The Solution, in Our View

By itself, instructional leadership is little more than a slogan, a blank bumper sticker. In some schools, principals follow all the recipes for instructional leadership: they review lesson plans, make brief visits in classrooms, check test scores, and circulate journal articles that give teachers tips, among dozens of other instructional activities that experts advise. Yet, they do not manage to create schoolwide conditions that encourage teacher collaboration, high standards for student work, and a climate where learning flourishes for students and teachers. Creating these conditions is the essence of instructional leadership. But it's tough work layered on top of principals' many other responsibilities.

Principals who are effective instructional leaders are catalysts; they do not follow a recipe. Instead, they aim to create a school environment where teachers feel supported and where students, parents, and teachers strive to achieve common goals and have a stake in helping one another do their best. Like teachers, they diagnose their school's conditions, including the strengths and weaknesses of their staffs, and figure out what actions are needed to move toward these goals. When all pull together, the chances of gains in test scores and other measures of academic achievement rise also.

PART THREE

Reforming Teaching and Learning

We began with the system of schooling, moved to school organization, and now turn to the classroom. Both system reform policies and changes in school organization indirectly influence what happens in classrooms. Curricular and instructional reformers have larger ambitions. They want to leave their imprint directly on classroom practice.

In this section, we analyze reforms that seek to shape what and how teachers teach and students learn. Topics that touch on the classroom spark considerable debate, which we find in examining reforms in reading, math, and teaching English language learners. Professional development, the key to actually changing what happens in classrooms, is included in the discussion, as is the use of technology for classroom instruction. We also look at how teachers are expected to use data to inform their instruction and alternative pathways for high school students that rely more on real-world projects.

16

Learning to Read— Phonics Revisited

SHOULD CHILDREN KNOW how to sound out words correctly, or should they understand what they are reading? Obviously, the answer is both, yet the so-called "reading wars" make it sound as if one must choose sides.

Phonics is the connection between written letters or letter combinations and how they sound. Some argue that until students master these connections—until they can decode letters into sounds, they cannot learn to read: first you learn the rules for sound-letter relationships, then you move to reading for understanding. Proponents of whole language, however, argue that reading is about making sense of the words, not simply sounding them out. They emphasize reading for understanding while teaching spelling and pronunciation along the way.

In fact, there are many effective ways to teach how letters and sounds are connected and many ways to teach reading comprehension. Still, many children do not learn to read.

Some children take to reading like a duck to water. Typically from well-educated parents in homes filled with books and conversation, these children will learn to read however it is taught. They start school with large vocabularies, and once they grasp the basic idea of correspondence between letters and sounds, they take off.

For those who start school with limited exposure to books and small vocabularies, however, learning to read is much more difficult. Or consider newcomers, speaking Spanish, Chinese, or one of dozens of other languages, trying to learn to read in English. It is difficult not only because of their backgrounds but also because English is a particularly complicated language. Unlike Spanish or French, English has many more sounds than letters, and the same sound can be spelled in different ways and different sounds can be spelled the same way. Try describing the rule for pronouncing *ou* or *gh,* as in *cough, through, though, tough, bough, dough.*

For too many children—even those who can pronounce all the words—the ability to understand what they read lags far behind their ability to sound out words. By fourth and fifth grades, when reading and thinking come together in the school curriculum, reading comprehension scores plummet. The problem gets worse as students who cannot read well reach middle and high school, where they are expected to make sense of textbooks in different subjects.

National data from 2009 suggest that only a third of the nation's fourth and eighth graders can be considered "proficient" in reading. Minority and poor children are much worse off. In addition, more than half of black and Hispanic fourth graders tested at the "below basic" level compared with less than a quarter of white students, according to the 2009 NAEP.[1]

This is the backdrop to the ongoing debate over how best to teach reading. The controversies are especially heated under NCLB because the federal government took sides by investing a billion dollars a year in its Reading First program, which promoted not only a phonics-based approach but, in particular, reading programs that are scripted, that literally tell elementary school teachers what to do and say at each step along the way.

Where Did the Idea of New Phonics Originate?

By the middle of the twentieth century, there were two main schools of thought on teaching reading: phonics and look-say. Look-say focused on recognizing words and what they mean rather than on the code that connects letters to sound. Some readers may remember "See Dick and Jane. See Dick and Jane run. See Spot. See Spot run."

Look-say was prevalent in the 1940s, 1950s, and 1960s and relied on books with very simple words. The 1970s and 1980s saw a return to phonics in many different forms, with claims that it was superior to look-say. Throughout the decades, most teachers actually used parts of both approaches. Most children learned to read well, and many did not. Whatever the popular approach of the day, those who struggled with reading tended to come from the least affluent homes with the least-educated parents.

In the 1980s and 1990s, the idea caught on that reading naturally develops if children are exposed to good books and guided to learn the sound-letter connections as they run into them. This whole language philosophy attracted strong adherents and vicious attackers. Advocates sported T-shirts making fun of the limitations of phonics: "Foniks rilly werks." Critics lambasted whole language for allowing students to make mistakes and to use "invented spelling" in their efforts to teach students to write before they could spell.

The twenty-first century brought a strong backlash against whole language. Critics used the federally supported National Reading Panel report as ammunition to justify both a return to phonics and use of scripted reading programs. Although the 2000 report itself was limited in scope and modest in its conclusions, the more broadly read summary and the rhetoric surrounding the report made claims about the connection between phonics-only instruction and learning to read that the report itself does not make.[2]

What Problem Is the New Phonics Intended to Solve?

Phonics-based instruction has the same goal as every other approach to reading: help children become literate adults. Whole language teachers are faulted for insufficient attention to phonics. Phonics teachers are faulted for inattention to how children make sense of the words and sentences they read. Each approach tries to compensate for the weaknesses of the other. But the problem remains: a high percentage of children cannot read, and most are from low-income, minority, and immigrant homes. So the root problem is how to teach children to read, especially those who start school behind their peers.

Reading specialists and researchers argue that the issue goes beyond whether one approach works better than another. In fact, along with teachers, most other experts reject the idea that one size fits all. The key question is how to figure out what *each* child needs to become a proficient reader. Researchers who look beneath test scores in reading find that struggling readers have quite different kinds of problems. So the underlying challenge is to pinpoint the stumbling blocks for each individual child.

Children who have trouble learning to read typically hit one or more of three main obstacles.[3] The first is understanding letter-sound relationships. The second is extracting meaning from what is read, which gets harder and harder as students advance through school. And the third is being motivated to want to read and understand.

Phonics instruction targets the first stumbling block head on. It begins to focus on the second, comprehension, but is criticized for reliance on simple-minded paragraphs and stories that do not require much thinking. Phonics-centric instruction is not designed to motivate interest in reading for children, but instead it intends to provide the skills needed to decode words.

To ensure that teachers provide adequate phonics-based instruction, federal officials and several state governments now push for elementary reading programs that dictate the details of each day's lesson, even providing an exact script for teachers to follow. Intended as a solution for poorly prepared and new teachers, such an approach contradicts the importance of diagnosing each child's particular needs. Such diagnosis, however, relies on teachers having the skills to act on the results.

Students need to grasp the fundamentals of reading by fourth grade so they can read and understand the progressively more difficult materials they encounter in their schoolwork. Yet, even those who master phonics are not necessarily able to handle the more complicated demands of reading in middle and high school courses. So, along with phonics, students need preparation for reading to learn. *Learning to read* and *reading to learn* are not the same. As one researcher noted, students who have no experience hearing ideas discussed can move through school without ever understanding what *understanding* is.[4] High school students who have not learned to read to learn are doomed to failure in most academic courses.

Does New Phonics Work?

National data on reading achievement suggest that whichever reading approach is in vogue makes little difference overall. NAEP scores for 2009 show little change in the last two decades in spite of the emphasis on education reform during this period. Reading reform in the 1990s shifted more toward whole language, while reforms in the 2000s emphasize phonics.

This does not mean that there are no better or worse ways to teach reading. Whether the emphasis is on phonics or comprehension, there is no one best way. The federally funded evaluation of its own Reading First found that the program increased time spent on reading instruction but had no consistent impact on reading skills and none at all on reading comprehension. [5]

Both phonics and comprehension are essential, and both can be done well or done poorly. Students drilled on phonics could sound out many words but have no idea what they had just said. At the same time, students who needed some basic rules of thumb to translate letters into sounds might never have gotten them in classrooms where poorly trained teachers went overboard on reading for pleasure.

Researchers and educators agree that it is important to focus on explicit phonics instruction in the early grades. But not at the expense of reading, being read to, and discussing words and stories. Like any sport, learning and practicing the individual skills is important. But if years go by without the student ever playing the game, interest quickly disappears. Imagine practicing dribbling and free throws without ever playing a basketball game. At the same time, throwing a youngster into a game before she has acquired any of the necessary skills could be overwhelming.

Government encouragement of scripted reading programs that emphasize phonics appears to solve one set of problems while causing still others. For new teachers, having a set of textbooks and guidelines for what to do and how fast to proceed through lessons can be an enormous help. As a top New York City administrator said. "Instead of everyone trying to figure out their own way in the classroom, which is the way these schools used to work, new teachers in particular need a very clearly defined program that isn't going to change with every new year . . . It's like learning to cook. You learn the basics first, and then you can get fancy."[6]

Yet such lock-step approaches fly in the face of one of the basic tenets of effective teaching: the need to identify where each student gets stuck. A team of nationally renowned reading experts analyzed reading difficulties in young children for the National Academy of Sciences and concluded: "If we have learned anything from this effort, it is that effective teachers are able to craft a special mix of instructional ingredients for every child they work with."[7]

Only a third of eighth graders are considered proficient in reading, according to 2009 NAEP data, and the fractions are half that for blacks and Hispanics. This discouraging picture suggests the need for solutions that go well beyond the federal emphasis on phonics in the early grades.

The Solution, in Our View

It turns out teaching reading *is* rocket science. Far from being a simple matter of connecting sounds and letters, reading is about understanding and thinking. Most teachers embrace the view that reading is key to all academic learning, and, as a result, they create hybrid reading lessons to balance the extreme positions. Educators know that children need the skills to break down a word and that phonics instruction is especially important for struggling readers. They also know that teaching phonics is relatively straightforward. Teaching understanding and thinking is not.

Balance in reading programs is equally important. Leaving it up to teachers to figure that out does not make sense—nor does telling teachers what to do every minute. Scripted programs may have their place, but most teachers need a better balance between direction on what, when, and how to teach and the flexibility to respond to the particular needs of individual students. Still, it does not make sense to leave all the work of achieving balance to teachers already pressed for time and, in some cases, without adequate training.

Thus, teachers need better training and better reading programs. They need opportunities to figure out which of many problems a particular student is having and get guidance on what to do. They also need experts to turn to for advice when they are not successful. At the same time, students from backgrounds where little reading occurs need preschool and other early-childhood experiences that introduce the concepts of reading and talking about ideas. They also need interesting books to read and the time to read for pleasure as they go through elementary school.

17

Reforming Math Teaching

"I'M NO GOOD at math." "I hate math!" How many students—and adults—make this claim? It is almost a badge of honor in this country. Perhaps it's not too surprising to find that large numbers of students fail algebra or, of those who pass, that many must enroll in remedial math in college.[1]

National test scores paint the same picture: 2008 NAEP results for high school students are virtually unchanged since the 1970s. Gaps remain large between white students and black and Hispanic students and have changed little since 1992.[2]

Instead of trying to understand why most students dislike math and fail to learn even the basics, ardent activists have waged public battles over how to teach math. On one side are the approaches favored by traditionalists, politely referred to as skills-based math but often derided as "parrot math" or "drill-and-kill" math. On the other side are programs favored by the reformers, politely referred to as reform- or standards-based math and frequently dismissed as "fuzzy math" or "anything-goes math."

While the labels make the two camps seem miles apart, both sides are actually in considerable agreement over what students need to know. Students, they say, need to master basic skills and procedures as well as understand underlying concepts. Without understanding the concepts, students have no way of knowing *when* to use a particular skill or formula (e.g., when they have to measure a room to estimate how much paint to buy or when they want to make sense of credit card interest charges).

What distinguishes the approaches from each other is how best to accomplish these goals. Both sides have extremists: those who believe that learning results from memorizing facts and formulas and those who believe that each child must develop his or her own understanding and procedures. But most educators, mathematicians, and the general public fall somewhere in the middle.

Where Did Idea of Reforming Math Teaching Originate?

The first wave of mathematics reform began in the early 1950s and accelerated after the Soviet Union's launch of the satellite Sputnik in 1957. The "new math" was created by university professors who aimed to update traditional mathematics content with newer ideas, such as set theory. This reform was short-lived. Some schools actually used new math materials, but many used traditional textbooks, which were reissued with new language—for example, replacing *answer* with *solution set*—that lent only the surface appearance of the new math. Few teachers had any knowledge of the new ideas, or opportunities to learn them, so their teaching remained the same. Those who did change were greeted by parent complaints that they had not learned math this way. So in the early 1970s, math teaching went "back to basics" with a vengeance.

After a decade of a traditional focus on computation and procedures, students were no better off. Most were neither good at problem-solving, which they had not been taught, nor at the basics, which they had been taught.

In 1983, *A Nation at Risk*'s scathing critique of public education prompted the National Council of Teachers of Mathematics (NCTM) to issue standards for mathematics curriculum in 1989. The goal was to shift the emphasis from teaching computation and procedures to teaching understanding of concepts and how to solve real-world problems. Learning by doing would replace rote learning. In a typical lesson, traditional math teachers state a rule, give an example, and then assign problems similar to the example. Reform math teachers, in contrast, might first provide students with a task and discuss the important mathematical ideas it embodies before giving students problems to solve. For example, to teach adding fractions, young students might be asked to figure out how seven people can share six cookies by cutting circles representing cookies into pieces. After several similar examples students would be asked to figure out the general rule for dividing any number of cookies among any number of people. The National Science Foundation supported the development of new programs based on ideas like these.

Criticized as going overboard with hands-on conceptual learning at the expense of mastering basic computational skills, the NCTM responded in 2006 with a new document containing grade-by-grade content standards that, even to its critics, was judged to restore balance between skills and understanding.

To justify the NCTM approach to teaching math, proponents of reform math point out how much both mathematics and the world have changed. More new mathematics has been developed in the past sixty years than the preceding thousands of years. And technology has also changed the way math is done by accountants and engineers as well as by mathematicians. Together with a greater understanding of how students learn, these historical developments form the rationale for reforming math teaching.

What Problem Is Reforming Math Teaching Intended to Solve?

Too many students fail to learn mathematics in school, and, for several decades, many students have viewed math as tedious at best. Dropouts point to math as their most discouraging school experience.[3] Almost everyone remembers sitting in a math class where the teacher goes over

EXAMPLES OF TRADITIONAL AND REFORM MATHEMATICS TEACHING

Traditional mathematics teaching

Teacher tells the class that pi is 3.14 (and maybe with many more decimal places). Then the teacher tells the class that the circumference of a circle is pi times the diameter. Students then practice calculating the circumferences of circles of different sizes.

Reform mathematics teaching

The teacher has students measure the diameter and circumference of a number of circles of different sizes. They record the data in two columns and begin to see a pattern—that the circumference is always a little over 3. Once they see that there is relationship, the teacher provides the name (pi) and the precise value.

homework, does a new problem, and assigns a page of problems. A few students "get it," but many do not. Robert Reys, who went on to become a mathematics professor, described his high school experience more than forty years ago: "Most of my peers hated math. Algorithms and tedious procedures were demonstrated with little or no explanation of why they work. Sensemaking and understanding were not a part of my experience of learning mathematics. Students left class thinking that math consisted only of dull procedures and rules to memorize."[4] Similar stories abound today. One student, forced to take remedial math at her community college, said, "My algebra teacher would give us an assignment and tell us to do the homework. The next day she would give answers on the overhead. I never understood how she did it, and she didn't show us."[5]

Today, understanding math is an essential part of being an informed citizen. In the past, adults could manage with minimal math skills. The need for math literacy in daily life is far greater than any time in the past. To make sense of poll results or claims made for new drugs; to file taxes or financial aid applications; or to know when you are being cheated all require the ability not only to calculate but also to think mathematically. Calculators can help with calculation—if the right numbers and operations are entered—but they don't help with sense-making.

In this context, reform math aims to increase the number of students who succeed at math, including raising the numbers of college-prep math courses taken by minority and low-income students.[6] To do so, proponents argue, requires changes in both what is taught and how it is taught. If the content is more closely tied to today's world and is taught in ways that foster understanding, then more students will learn more math.

Does Reform Math Teaching Work?

It is easier to show that traditional math teaching does not work than it is to prove that reform math teaching works. The failure of minority and low-income students to succeed in math and the need for so many students to take remedial math in college demonstrate that traditional approaches are failing. Watching young people try to make change without a cash register that computes the answer is enough to convince most Americans that students are not learning math.

Studies that contrast different types of math instruction point to benefits of reform-oriented math teaching. Researchers find that students have better results on tests of problem solving and no worse on computation tests than those in traditional math programs.[7] A rigorous study randomly assigned first-grade teachers to a month-long workshop on how children develop problem-solving skills in addition and subtraction. Compared to the control group, these teachers encouraged students to use a variety of problem-solving strategies and taught number facts significantly less, yet these students outperformed those in control classes on number facts as well as in problem solving and self-confidence in their problem-solving abilities.[8]

Recent studies confirm the obvious: the more math content that teachers know, the better their students do.[9] But such studies also emphasize the need to know more than math; they also need to know something about how students learn math and how to teach different mathematical concepts and procedures. The implications are clear but have gone unheeded. Most elementary school teachers have little background in math. A case in point: nearly three-quarters of aspiring elementary teachers failed the math section on the Massachusetts teacher licensing exam in 2009.[10] Meanwhile, middle and high school teachers with math backgrounds are in short supply. And in urban high schools the turnover rate among math teachers is high, leaving most students in classrooms with inexperienced teachers.

While the choice of curriculum and textbooks can make teaching easier or harder, the bottom line is that the teacher matters more than the program or book. Good teachers who know math well can work with a traditional math textbook and also use activities that help students discover what concepts like area and perimeter mean. Good teachers can make connections to the real world and across different topics. They can also use a reform math program and augment its activities with practice in computation to build speed.

But what about teachers without the strongest math or teaching skills? "I strongly believe that the most crucial step for promoting racial equality in this country is to educate all elementary teachers mathematically," Patricia Clark Kenschaft, a professor of mathematics at Montclair State University, said in 2005, pointing to research suggesting that at least some of the gap between black and white elementary students can be traced to differences in their teachers' mathematical knowledge.[11] She describes working with a group of third-grade teachers who did not know the relationship between multiplication and area. In fact, to her astonishment, they did not even know how to calculate the area of a rectangle. After teaching them area and demonstrating that 3 x 5 can be represented as a rectangle with sides of 3 and 5, the teachers wondered why no one had told them this "secret" before.[12]

Proponents of reform math claim that reform programs make it possible for teachers to learn more math themselves just from using the materials. However, the authors are presuming that teachers will follow the books closely, though most teachers do not; they pick and choose what makes sense to them. That most elementary school teachers end up with a blend of traditional and reform math is not surprising.[13] But it frustrates both traditionalists and reformers who rightly fear that students are missing out on important facts and ideas.

Both traditionalists and reformers are also trapped by the sheer number of topics they must teach to cover all the state standards likely to be on the test. The proliferation of standards and the need for textbook publishers to include them all has contributed to the most common critique of math courses in the United States: "A mile wide and an inch deep."

A 2008 government-sponsored report and a draft of common-core standards released in early 2010 attempt to narrow the topics.[14] But critics argue that narrowing the elementary curriculum to arithmetic facts and procedures, with a little geometry thrown in, will not lead to depth of understanding. Signs of battle are on the horizon. As one newspaper headline warned, reporting on the common-core standards, "'Math Wars' over National Standards May Erupt Again in California."[15]

All in all, whether reforming math teaching works is answered only in small part by researchers. The full answer is that it can work if teachers are well-prepared and have the support of their colleagues and if political battles do not detract from these goals.

The Solution, in Our View

Without question, most elementary school teachers need to know more math—and teachers at all levels need to know more about teaching math. If students are not exposed at all to ideas like functions and probability in elementary school, they are unlikely to survive high school math courses. Reform math programs are designed to help teachers learn as well as teach these ideas *if* they have high-quality training available and expert teachers to consult.

Math knowledge alone, however, is not enough. Teachers need to know a variety of ways to explain both procedures and concepts that are essential for later high school math courses. Teachers at both the elementary and secondary level need to know how to check for understanding through questioning and assessments that go beyond asking for right answers. Teachers also need to entice students to become interested in math in a world full of distractions. Given the importance and difficulty of teaching math well, even to first graders, it's worth seriously considering hiring elementary math specialists to do the job, sparing math-phobic teachers from playing that role.

Characterizing traditional math as rote learning and reform math as learning by doing does not do justice to either. Neither is sufficient for students to grasp underlying ideas. At the same time, moving from grade to grade without facility in computation is a serious handicap for students regardless of their conceptual understanding. Opportunities at school and community centers to practice skills using appealing computer games could help bolster these skills outside of class time.

Current tests and textbooks contribute to maintaining the status quo in math. The questions on standardized tests and the topics they cover match traditional textbooks and course descriptions. For example, students who took reformed math courses that integrated algebra and geometry over two years instead of two separate courses have been known to face an algebra-only test that at the end of the first year included topics not yet covered. More adaptable test practices are needed.

Trading breadth for depth is critical, but guaranteeing the depth side of the equation is easier said than done. Unless textbooks and tests focus on fewer topics and more on mathematical thinking, teachers will continue to struggle to cover the material, and students will continue to lose out.

18

English Language Learning

WHAT IS THE best way for non-English-speaking children to become fluent in English and successful in school? Arguments have raged over this seemingly straightforward question for decades. Should there be classrooms where teachers speak only English and all materials are in English? Or should there be classrooms where students and teachers speak in the students' native language and use materials in their language while adding more and more English over the years? Or should there be classrooms where students and teachers switch back and forth from English to the students' native language during lessons? Policymakers, researchers, parents, and teachers all want answers to these questions.

Whichever strategy is used, the next question is, How long does it take? Non-English speakers can pick up casual conversational English quickly, but that's not the same as reading at grade level or knowing the academic English needed to learn math, science, social studies, and literature. And the hardest question of all is, Can English language learners (ELLs) maintain the same level of achievement with other students as they become fluent in English?

These are all important questions, because in 2006 nearly 5.5 million public schoolchildren, about one in ten, needed help to become fluent in English. Most ELLs are Spanish-speaking children (75 percent), with Chinese and Vietnamese next highest in percentages. And most—almost three-quarters—were born in the United States and are U.S. citizens. By 2025, some experts predict that the rapidly growing population of ELLs will make up 25 percent of public school enrollment.[1]

Bilingual education, in which students are taught in both English and their native language, and English immersion, or sheltered English, in which students are taught only in English, provide competing approaches to helping non-English-speaking students learn the language. Reformers of different stripes promote each approach, but their arguments are based more on ideology than data.

Yet, the questions are urgent because fluency in English is strongly linked to staying in school. Among Hispanics born outside of the United States, 43 percent left school before graduating in 2001, with even higher percentages in urban high schools. Because dropouts are more likely to be unemployed and involved in crime, reducing the dropout rate is crucial to the lifetime success of ELLs.[2]

Where Did the Idea of Bilingual Versus English-Only Education Originate?

Initially, American schools offered only one answer to these questions: sink or swim. Elementary school teacher Sam Anaya recalled entering kindergarten years earlier in Oklahoma speaking only Spanish: "I was just thrown in."[3]

For decades, schools placed immigrants into regular English-only classrooms without any language assistance; many districts even banned the use of Spanish in and out of class. Those immigrant children who picked up English swiftly and kept up with their studies survived.

One newcomer recalled arriving in the United States from Germany at the age of nine knowing only two words, *yes* and *no*. After being put into the fourth grade with a few other non-English-speaking students, he recalled that "after a year of regular schooling we were almost indistinguishable from our native American peers—this despite the fact that most of our parents spoke very little English." Although the German immigrant and Spanish-speaking Anaya eventually "swam"—Anaya became a teacher and taught at the school he once attended—many immigrants "sunk" and dropped out of school.[4]

The teaching of English to immigrants has a long history which makes clear that the issue is as much political as educational. In early nineteenth-century public schools, English was the only language of instruction for native and immigrant children. As more and more non-English-speaking immigrants came to America and sent their children to school, some groups objected. In 1840, German immigrants successfully lobbied the Ohio legislature to pass a law requiring local school boards to offer German in public schools whenever seventy-five taxpayers demanded it in writing. In Cincinnati, public schools were established where English and German were the languages of instruction in reading, grammar, and spelling in the primary grades moving on to instruction in English in geography, math, and other subjects. By 1899, there were nearly fifteen thousand primary grade students splitting their week evenly between a German teacher and an English teacher.[5]

Between the mid-nineteenth and early twentieth centuries, Polish, Italian, Spanish, and other ethnic groups used their votes to secure instruction in their language or to establish formal study of their languages in school.

That ethnic willingness to foster bilingualism politically, however, was challenged repeatedly by native-born Americans after strong surges of immigration (1880–1920) and during economic depressions (1890–1910) that raised fears of competition for jobs. Worries over being swamped by foreign cultures not only led to anti-immigration laws and occasional riots against newcomers but also to changes in school policies.

Political and business elites believed that the nation was a melting pot in which immigrants gave up their culture and were fused into Americans as they worked, worshiped, played sports, voted, and went to school. The melting pot idea clearly implied English as the only language of instruction. The sink-or-swim approach became daily practice in classrooms.[6]

Yet, losing one's native language and culture in order to become American caused tension between immigrant parents and their children. Surely, parents knew that learning English was essential for their children to succeed in the nation that had welcomed them, but many immigrants regretted, even hated, seeing children and grandchildren no longer speaking their native tongue or engaging in traditional cultural practices. For decades that seemed to be the only choice—abandon one's language and culture to gain another. While cultural pluralism—accepting ethnic and language differences—grew in the 1930s, not until the civil rights movement of the 1960s did an alternative arise that renewed an older but forgotten tradition: bilingualism.

Pressures from civil rights groups led Congress to pass the Bilingual Education Act in 1968. The law funded experimental transitional bilingual programs that placed children from poor families not fluent in English into special basic skill classes in which they would use their native languages to keep up with reading, math, and other subjects while they were taught enough English to eventually transfer to regular classrooms. A decade later, the U.S. Office of Education was funding 425 projects in sixty-eight different languages. The vast majority (80 percent), though, were in Spanish. At that time critics charged that bilingual education kept ELL children already fluent in English in special classrooms to maintain language and culture and to keep jobs for bilingual aides and teachers.[7]

By the late 1970s, after a decade of transitional bilingual programs, neither policymakers nor researchers could offer clear evidence that this approach was, indeed, the best way to teach English language learners. Nor could they determine how long it would take for nonnative speakers to acquire both conversational and academic English, and thus ensure academic achievement equal to native speakers of English. Even after the U.S. Supreme Court ruled in *Lau v. Nichols* in 1974 that school districts must provide special instruction to children with a home language other than English, the decision did not specify what the instruction should be.

Since the 1960s, state and federal laws have provided alternatives through English as a Second Language (ESL), Sheltered English, and dual immersion programs, in addition to bilingual education. Most recently, to hold states and school districts accountable for helping nonnative speakers progress academically and to lower the dropout rate, NCLB requires districts to make "adequate yearly progress"—as measured by test scores—with ELLs. Pressure to prepare ELLs for tests to meet prescribed academic standards has pushed schools to rely on ESL, Sheltered English, and English-only techniques, rather than bilingual programs, to teach reading and math. Today, as they have done for well over a century and a half, policymakers, practitioners, parents, and voters continue to debate these alternatives.[8]

What Problem Is Reforming English Language Learning Intended to Solve?

Teachers of ELL students face a daunting task. They can have a few to an entire classroom of non-English-speaking children of varying abilities and school experiences. Some are literate in their native languages; many are not. They must help these students learn English vocabulary, syntax, grammar, and pronunciation while teaching them to read and do math proficiently.

At the same time, the federal NCLB law requires that this group of students meet standards each year and make progress toward closing the achievement gap with their English-speaking peers.[9] But how do you both teach a new language and maintain the same, let alone faster, rate of progress as students already fluent in English? As one Arizona elementary ELL immersion teacher said in 2003 on the passage of a state law banning bilingual and ESL programs, "The idea is not to water down the curriculum, but the reality is the curriculum is watered down because students are just trying to learn the language."[10]

For immigrant children who start school in kindergarten and move through the grades with help in learning English, progress in language development is evident. But many students enter their first U.S. school at higher grade levels, even high school, thus rendering the challenge even greater.

Because educating English learners intersects with immigration politics, decisions about how to teach ELLs must also solve political challenges. For example, in 1998 enough Californians signed petitions to put Proposition 227 on the statewide ballot, requiring all instruction in public schools to be in English. Under Proposition 227, children not fluent in English would receive only one year of Sheltered English. A waiver could be granted permitting bilingual instruction if parents wanted it. The referendum passed with 61 percent of the vote. A similar proposition also passed in Arizona (63 percent) in 2000 banning bilingual instruction except for students already fluent in English.[11] Even with this massive backlash against it, bilingual instruction continues under waivers in California and many other states as a way of educating ELLs because some policymakers, researchers, educators, and parents do find the available evidence convincing.

Do Current Approaches to Teaching English Learners Work?

Current approaches to ELL instruction cover the waterfront. Out of every hundred ELL students, sixty are in English-only classrooms and forty-eight of those get some amount of help with language learning. The other forty are in classrooms that use their native language, but how much and for how long differs from one school to the next.[12]

The current consensus among researchers who have slowly accumulated studies in the United States and Canada is that almost any program with some support for language instruction done well can be effective—but only up to a point and only for some students. For elementary school children in reading, math, and other subjects, programs carried out with experienced teachers who carefully and systematically teach the language and the material will result in ELLs becoming conversant in English within two to three years.[13]

However, conversational English is not the same as the academic English needed for each subject area. For Spanish-speaking students to match native speakers in academic English, it takes at least four to seven years of work in ESL and bilingual classrooms, rather than English-only ones.[14]

When programs provide insufficient help or end too soon, which is all too common, collateral damage occurs. Whether the approach

COMMON ELL PROGRAMS

Transitional bilingual education. Programs in which teachers are fluent both in English and students' native language that are designated for students who are learning to speak English.

English as a Second Language (ESL). Programs, often separate classes or pull-outs, are conducted mostly in English, but teachers can use native language of students when needed if possible.

Sheltered English. Programs—often part of an English-only approach—are short term (usually no more than one year) and designed to make content more accessible to English learners. They are conducted in English, with some help for those learning the language for the first time.

English immersion. Classroom lessons are in simple English so that students can learn the language and academic subjects. In some districts, teachers use English 70 percent of the time and work up to 95–100 percent in English by the end of the program.

Dual immersion. Programs where instruction is in English and another language are open to students fluent in English who want to learn another language and to native speakers of the other language.

is English-only with extra help or language support in the classroom for ELLs, when teachers are poorly trained, or when ESL or bilingual programs terminate language help in one to three years, most ELLs fall steadily behind academically.[15]

Similarly, Sheltered English and English-only programs often provide insufficient help and last only one or two years. Not surprisingly, both the achievement gap and the high dropout rate among Hispanic students, according to researchers, are linked to the amount and quality of language instruction children receive early in their school careers.

Although there is no research consensus on particular programmatic approaches, many researchers find some points of agreement.

One is that if you learn to read in your native language, you will have an easier time learning to read in a new language. Or, more broadly, the higher the level of a student's literacy, the easier it is to learn a second language. Another is that good instruction is good instruction, whether for ELLs or other students—in particular, combining interactive and direct instruction, including, for example, structured discussions. Opportunities for conversation are particularly important both for what ELLs learn and for providing teachers with a window into their language and subject matter knowledge.[16]

Because bilingual and English-only education continue to be politicized, there will likely be multiple approaches to instructing ELLs for the immediate future. Research evidence will take a back seat. Overheated public debates will need to chill before research and experienced educators' judgments can be brought to bear on the worth of bilingual education.

The Solution, in Our View

In the hands of knowledgeable and skilled teachers for extended periods of time, bilingual education is demonstrably effective in teaching reading, math, and other subjects to English language learners. However, there are too few skilled teachers, and the problem is unlikely to be solved in the near future. Similarly, teachers in English-only and Sheltered English programs need far more training in communicating efficiently with their ELLs if the students are to have a chance to move beyond conversational English to master the language they need to succeed in their academic subjects.

The distinction between conversational and academic language is often overlooked or misunderstood by educators and the public. Educators and parents need help in realizing that conversational English is not enough to succeed academically. Teachers in schools with high proportions of non-English speakers need to learn how to help students with their language development. Parents and their children need opportunities beyond the school day to learn English.

Yet, even if bilingual education and English-only programs were to lose the taint of their political past, more would be needed than qualified teachers and solid instruction. The majority of English learners carry the added weight of poverty and family illiteracy. Their challenge is not simply one of learning a new language. To help ELLs grow intellectually, socially, psychologically, and emotionally, public schools have to do much more than provide effective bilingual and Sheltered English teachers.

To make children and youth both fluent in English and academically strong enough to continue and complete school, they need more time. The job of the schools must expand to include preschool, an extended school day, summer programs, and efforts to involve parents in educating their children. Moreover, efforts are needed that remove the stigma of poverty attached to bilingual education and instead use the strengths that children bring to school. Like most reforms aimed at those in low-income families, schools cannot do the job alone.[17]

19

Redesigning Professional Development

ASKED ABOUT HER experience in a week-long summer institute performing experiments in physics, a middle school teacher announced, "This is much better than professional development."[1] Almost a dirty word among teachers and parents alike, professional development, teacher in-service, staff development, training—whatever the label—has come to mean wasted hours spent in "spray and pray" or "sit 'n' git" workshops. Teachers traipse across town to listen to an inspirational speech or presentation on the latest hot topic. Worse yet, school is out for a half-day or a full day sending parents scrambling for child care.

The idea that professional development is supposed to be valuable continuing education for teachers somehow fell by the wayside. Yet today it may be more important than ever. Schools are under the gun to raise student achievement, which can happen only if teachers learn to improve what they do. As former U.S. Secretary of Education Margaret Spellings put it, "If all you ever do is all you've ever done, then all you'll ever get is all you've ever got!"[2]

So the question is, How do teachers get better? Testing and accountability put pressure on educators to improve, but this pressure has to translate into strategies for helping students learn more. Analyzing test scores is one thing; knowing what to do to increase them is another. In theory, high-quality professional development should help by arming teachers with more knowledge and skills about the subjects they teach and about how students learn.

The reform view of professional development is the opposite of the one-shot workshop. Professional development is now expected to combine intensive summer institutes that bring teachers up to date on content and understanding with a variety of on-the-job opportunities during the school year for learning and help. It is based on the idea that teachers, like other professionals, learn from each other as well as from experts. Instead of always leaving the school for workshops or courses, reformed professional development aims to create teacher learning communities in schools, bolstered by chances to observe master teachers and get help in the classroom from expert coaches.

Where Did These Ideas for Professional Development Originate?

Professional development for teachers in the nineteenth century was not radically different from much of what is provided today. Superintendents or outside experts offered classes, gave presentations, and ran summer institutes to help teachers pass required tests and improve their skills. These were held in a central location and resembled many of today's one-shot workshops. The people running the system were the ones who decided what teachers needed.

By the 1950s, colleges and universities, as well as school district offices, became the major providers of professional development, continuing the practice of deciding the content from above. Districts typically required the participation of all teachers in some activities, usually presentations about new policies and requirements; other alternatives, such as university courses, were left up to individual teachers who chose from a menu of offerings.

Over the past two decades new ideas about how to make professional development worthwhile have multiplied. The impetus for professional development reform comes from several sources. One has been the need to justify investments in continuing education for teachers. When parents run into teachers in the grocery store on staff development day or hear from teachers how boring it is, legislators, who are quick to slash funds for professional development, hear about it. Little documentation of the effect of professional development on teachers and students, combined with a few horror stories, makes it an easy hit for budget cuts.

Another impetus is the fact that there is a lot more knowledge about teaching and learning today than when many teachers received their college degrees. Teachers are also being asked to teach new topics. In the past, fifth-grade teachers were not expected to introduce concepts in algebra and probability. Today they are.

Current ideas about professional development also borrow from the world of business, where on-the-job training is an integral feature of companies looking to improve their workforce. If a company adopts a new method or procedure, all the affected employees are sent off for training to retool, often for weeks at a time. Districts and schools have not made these kinds of investments in the past.

The No Child Left Behind Act has thrown some of its weight behind professional development. Not only are teachers under pressure to improve test scores, but the law also requires districts to spend at least 5 percent of their Title I budgets on high-quality professional development. In turn, districts must require each school in need of improvement to spend 10 percent of their Title I budget on professional development. In fact, the law provides a list of the kinds of activities that would be considered high quality. Included are several buzzwords that contrast with the one-shot workshop approach: "sustained, intensive, and classroom focused."

Specific recommendations for improving professional development have been influenced by studies of best practices in successful schools, districts, and countries. For example, one district in New York City raised achievement scores by creating a rich and varied districtwide system of professional development. Each school had literacy coaches who worked with teachers and conducted regular classroom walk-throughs as a basis for identifying teachers' weaknesses and matching them with appropriate help and training.[3] The publicity surrounding this success story spawned national interest in coaching for teachers and classroom walk-throughs by principals.

Similarly, wide publicity of studies of teaching in other countries, most notably Japan, popularized the idea of professional learning communities in which groups of teachers in a school meet regularly to discuss lessons and continually sharpen their instructional skills.[4]

Pressure to create more effective professional development converged with studies that have identified critical elements and resulted in a long list of essentials. The list conjures up an image of a teacher enrolled in redesigned university courses, attending one-week or longer summer institutes, observing master teaching for extended periods of time, meeting regularly with colleagues to analyze data and discuss lessons and how to improve them, holding frequent discussions with a school coach or mentor, and receiving feedback from the principal and colleagues. In practice, most professional development falls far short of this imagined scenario.

What Problem Is Redesigned Professional Development Intended to Solve?

In the big picture, the goal of better teacher professional development is to improve teaching and therefore increase student achievement. Policymakers and reformers now look to professional development as the way to arm teachers with the know-how they need to help all their students learn more. What this amounts to in practice is creating worthwhile learning opportunities for teachers, overcoming the view of professional development as a waste of time, and figuring out how to provide the kind of time and help teachers need to learn and put new ideas into practice.

Under increasing pressure to raise student achievement, teachers have few on-the-job opportunities to learn how to get better. Most teachers spend their workday in a classroom with students. They have little chance to meet with other teachers beyond official faculty meetings. Reform ideas for professional development are intended to overcome the current weaknesses of teacher training, classroom isolation, and traditional professional development.

One such weakness is the separation of much teacher preparation and professional development from the classroom. Reformers argue that teachers need ongoing opportunities to improve what they do, and that this can only happen if teachers work together as professional communities. The idea is that teachers who teach the same grade or subject meet regularly to look at data from their students and discuss how better to teach a particular topic or concept. Such communities are intended to bring teachers out from behind closed classroom doors and make their work more visible to each other.

Another weakness is the one-shot approach. New approaches are expected to be more sustained and employ intensive courses or week-long institutes. Yet another weakness is the lack of just-in-time, on-site help for teachers—efforts to observe and give feedback as teachers try something new in the classroom. This approach necessitates having coaches or mentors at the school.

A further weakness of traditional professional development is its generic nature: workshops about how to group students or how to implement a new discipline policy or how to write good lesson plans. Reformers urge a focus on the subject-matter concepts teachers teach coupled with how students learn them. Formerly, districts offered professional development as a menu of choices from which teachers could choose to fit their desires or schedules. Now, reformers urge attention to school goals and priorities set by the school or district.

Together, the reform view of professional development focuses the content on what teachers need to know and do and locates the activities in the school where teachers can work together and get help to improve their teaching.

Does Redesigned Professional
Development Work?

Whether professional development works or not can be considered in different ways. Is it possible to create the kinds of professional development envisioned by reformers? If so, does it change what teachers know

TEACHERS LEARNING TOGETHER

At Paterson School 2, a low-income K–8 school in New Jersey's urban Paterson district, teachers meet weekly in small groups, thanks to clever scheduling by the principal. But the meetings are far from typical team meetings. Paterson teachers are using an idea borrowed from Japan: lesson study. Every twelve weeks they tackle a unit in mathematics. Teachers study the ideas and how the textbook presents them and how they connect to other lessons and grade levels.

Teachers develop lessons and try them out, sharing what works and what does not in their meetings. They observe each other and record their thinking and what they learned and keep these observations and videotaped lessons for future reference. "It's the greatest thing I've ever done personally as professional development," said William C. Jackson, the school's full-time math facilitator.

Like a growing number of teacher learning communities, these teachers focus on a specific goal, decide what data will best capture student learning, observe each other, and discuss their observations and student data, which inform their future classroom actions. These teachers open up their classrooms for analysis—a gutsy move for professionals who have spent their careers behind closed doors. Afterward, they discuss how the lesson went. They might debate whether fifth graders are old enough to understand measurement error or simply tell a new teacher that she needs to talk more slowly or point out a concept that several students did not understand. Teachers not only learn but also immediately put to practice what they have learned.

SOURCES

Lewis, Catherine C., Rebecca Perry, Jacqueline Hurd, and Mary Pat O'Connell. "Lesson Study Comes of Age in North America." *Phi Delta Kappan* 88, no. 04 (2006): 273–281.

Viadero, Debra. "In 'Lesson Study' Sessions, Teachers Polish Their Craft." *Education Week,* February 11, 2004, 8.

and do? And, if so, does it increase what students learn? If the answer is still *yes,* is that learning measured by an annual standardized test?

Given this chain of logic, it is hardly surprising that little evidence exists that even high-quality professional development alters what teachers do or raises test scores. If a teacher goes to a two-hour workshop on teaching statistics to fifth graders, no one would expect her to immediately change how she teaches or for her students' test scores to jump immediately as a result.

However, suppose a district invests substantial money over several years in classes that help fifth-grade teachers better understand probability and statistics and how students learn these concepts and, moreover, that these teachers discuss what they have learned and figure out classroom activities they could use in their weekly learning teams. Then it makes sense to ask if, overall, teachers have changed their usual teaching practices and if scores have increased on a test designed to measure the concepts teachers were taught.

Only a few studies have tried to link professional development to altered teaching practices and student learning. Teachers' language skills and knowledge of the subject seem to make the biggest difference in how much students learn.[5] It makes sense that students would learn more from teachers who can explain well and who understand the concepts enough to answer students' questions and respond with many different examples. Other research finds that the types of formal professional development that influenced student learning the most were those that taught teachers more about the subject itself and about how students learn the concepts that were taught. This mattered more than whether it happened at the school, included classroom visits, or involved teachers working together.[6]

But these studies are few, they mostly looked at math and science, and the links to student outcomes are weak. The impact of professional development on test scores is more likely to show up if a test measures exactly what teachers were expected to learn rather than broad assessments of student achievement.

A growing body of evidence suggests that teachers can learn from each other, both from coaching and collaborating in professional learning communities. For example, a recent study of coaching of early-grade teachers found a substantial impact on teacher expertise and student learning that increased over the years and was higher for those with more coaching.[7]

Recent studies of professional learning communities where teachers work together regularly on instructional problems find not only increases in student achievement but also changes in school and classroom environments. Researchers do not claim causal relationships but document that students have higher achievement in schools characterized by teacher collaboration. Moreover, teachers and students in such schools develop a sense of collective responsibility for each other's learning.[8]

But such communities are hard to build and sustain. Among other things, they require regularly scheduled time for teachers to meet and as well as support from school leadership—conditions that are rare, especially in urban districts. And they need strong teacher leaders and structured protocols that help teachers stay focused on important questions; otherwise, the more immediate demands of the job become the topic of conversation.[9]

Researchers also point to the challenges in mounting good professional development programs for teachers. Whether they're discussing statistics or culture or writing, those who teach teachers need to know the concepts well, know how students learn them, and know how to teach adults. This is a tall order, one that the majority of providers of professional development are unable to meet.

Even with high-quality providers of professional development, teachers are not necessarily attracted to such opportunities. Not surprisingly, many bristle at the implication that their own knowledge is lacking. Moreover, with ever-increasing pressure to raise test scores, teachers, often under direction from their superiors, seek quick fixes, not deeper understanding of what they teach.

The Solution, in Our View

The oft-cited report *A Nation at Risk* recommended that "school boards should adopt an 11-month contract for teachers. This would ensure time for curriculum and professional development, programs for students with special needs, and a more adequate level of teacher compensation."[10] Of course, this would require a substantial increase in education budgets. The alternative is to reduce the time teachers spend with students. In European and Asian nations with high test scores, teachers spend fifteen to twenty-five hours per week, roughly half of their total work time, collaborating on curriculum and instruction and participating in professional development. This compares to three to five hours a week for U.S. teachers, who spend almost their entire day with students.[11] Yet, without major changes in the time teachers have for anything other than teaching itself, it is hard to imagine when teachers would take courses and work together to figure out why some students are not learning.

It takes more than just setting aside time for professional development to be worthwhile. Without effective teachers of teachers and well-trained mentors, for example, professional development will not provide much bang for the buck. Without strong teacher leadership and principal support, teacher professional communities will not flourish. Teachers, too, need incentives to reach beyond their current level of expertise. Current priorities are to raise test scores quickly, which works against the ideas embodied in professional development reform.

What is clear is that improvements in student learning are anchored in teacher learning. Without high-quality professional development, broadly defined, neither is likely to occur.

20

High-Tech Classrooms

Mrs. Johnson's fifth graders have their eyes glued to the front of the room as she stands in front of the class with her pointer aimed at the center of an erupting volcano. What used to be a blackboard is now a whiteboard able to display the Web site she has accessed on her computer. The classroom discussion about the density, color, and speed of lava flows is no longer a purely theoretical one. Students are about to turn to their laptops to begin their reports with access to several Web sites on volcanoes. Sifting through information and organizing their thoughts is still difficult, but the work of gathering information and producing written text is vastly richer and more efficient than it used to be.

In Mr. Rodriguez's world history class, pairs of students are creating, designing, and writing travel brochures and news releases for tourists visiting Latin America as a two-week project describing and analyzing different countries' geographies, economies, governments, religions, and cultures. For three consecutive class periods, student teams use laptops from a mobile cart to find information and photos for Costa Rica, Bolivia, Argentina, and other countries. With wireless access to the Internet and desk-top publishing software, some teams have already artfully designed informative brochures, articles, and even comic strips about each country.

These composite views of different classrooms suggest how teachers have adapted new technologies to enhance daily lessons. The combination of today's powerful laptop computers and the vast resources of the Internet were just barely on the horizon fifteen years ago. Individual examples of powerful uses of portable electronic devices abound, as do hopes that technology can do what has been beyond the grasp of earlier classrooms reforms: increase teacher efficiency and effectiveness and student motivation and learning.

Yet even as imaginative uses of technology increase yearly, laptops, interactive whiteboards, and hand-held devices have yet to become routine in most classrooms across the nation. In spite of abundant numbers of high-tech equipment in schools and almost universal access to the Internet, daily use of these devices in lessons still remains the exception. And even where they are used, student performance has not skyrocketed. Why is this, and what's the prognosis for the short run and the long run?[1]

Where Did the Idea Originate?

Expecting technology to solve a host of education problems has a long and dismal history. From film projectors early in the twentieth century to television and then computers, reformers dreamed that these new technologies would revolutionize teaching and learning. Not only would students be more motivated by the entertainment value of the new media, they would learn more with greater efficiency. But the anticipated revolution from use of technology did not pan out. Film projectors languished in closets; televisions and videocassette recorders sat in classroom corners, occasionally used.

The advent of personal computers and powerful software in the 1980s offered a whole new array of possible educational uses, from word processing to arithmetic drill and practice. However, it was the arrival of portability and Internet access in the past decade that has transformed the vision of technology from that of performing traditional tasks more efficiently to making fundamental shifts in what is taught and how it is learned. Now students can travel on a virtual spaceship to see different views of the planets; they can even control a camera on the space shuttle by tracking the shuttle's orbital path and selecting points on Earth to photograph, images that are then posted on the Web.

Policymakers, business leaders, educators, and, of course, vendors share some version of this vision. The federal government, states, and districts have invested billions of dollars in wiring schools and purchasing laptops, hand-held devices, and interactive white boards to provide each and every student with Internet access and new ways of learning and teaching. Policymakers and business leaders tout the virtues of new technologies and entice schools with donations of hardware and software and occasional training on their use. All the enticements and investments are aimed at getting teachers and students to routinely use these technologies in daily lessons.[2]

What Problems Do New Technologies Intend to Solve?

Reformers believe laptops, hand-held computers/mobile phones, and interactive whiteboards can transform teaching and learning. From software with simulations of science experiments to drill-and-practice games, these classroom technologies can, in theory, provide new opportunities for student learning and end decades of passive, teacher-directed classrooms.

Reformers also believe that these devices can help teachers become more productive through electronic versions of grade books, report cards, attendance taking, and other time-consuming record-keeping tasks. The time saved can be spent on activities directly related to teaching. Moreover, with laptops and easy access to the Internet, teachers can access an infinite variety of ideas and resources for preparing exciting lessons.

The same kinds of productivity tools used in the business world can also help students be more efficient. Word processing enables more editing of writing as well as neater reports with correct spelling. Graphing calculators replace the tedium of plotting points on paper, helping students focus on the big concepts instead of the mechanics.

Whatever their application, students who use these devices become familiar with common workplace and learning tools, which could be particularly advantageous for students who might not have access to the latest technologies at home.[3] Using high-tech tools on a daily basis in classrooms is expected to end student boredom, open up a world of information, prepare students for the workplace, and transform teaching—problems that have plagued schools for a century.

Does Access to These New Technologies Work?

Not yet. Schools have deployed laptops and hand-held devices in labs, media centers, and classrooms. Interactive whiteboards (IWB) have been installed in hundreds of thousands of classrooms. Nationally the presence of computers jumped from one computer for every 125 students in the mid-1980s to one computer for every four students in 2007.[4] In 2009, 85 percent of districts reported that they have schools and classrooms with IWBs.[5] As for laptops, 25 percent of districts said that they have one or more schools with a laptop for every student.[6] Although the presence of computers, especially laptops, and whiteboards in schools has increased dramatically in the past decade, uses are neither as widespread nor as revolutionary as expected.

For every story touting teacher and student use of laptops or IWBs, there are stories of limited use. For every Denver School of Technology and Science using 1:1 laptops for Internet simulations, creating student collaboration, and digital drop boxes, there is a Louisville, Kentucky.[7] After spending $30 million on computer technology, two-thirds to three-quarters of the teachers in Louisville do not regularly use computers in their lessons, according to the district director of technology.[8] Similarly, a report on uses of technology in Chicago's public schools noted that such use is "at a rudimentary level" and that "most schools have not substantially integrated technology into students' coursework," in spite of the fact that most students and teachers believe that using computers and the Internet brings academic and occupational advantages.[9]

The hope that the potential of the Internet and portability would radically change how teachers teach remains a hope. In fact, where technology is used, it tends to be used to support the kind of teaching already in place. Several studies have shown that teachers of middle-class students are far more likely to use technology to enhance thinking through simulations and applications in contrast to drill and practice for low-income and minority students.[10]

Although some teachers' tasks are more efficient with computers, these efficiencies do not necessarily translate into more attention to students. And overall there is scant evidence that computer use per se results in higher test scores.

Today's students know how to download music files, send e-mail and instant messages, and use search engines, but they don't know how to read and think critically—skills all the more important as the Internet becomes their main source of information. According to Lorie Roth, a California State University administrator, "Every single [student] that comes through the door thinks that if you just go to Google and get some hits—you've got material for your research paper right there."[11]

Wireless hand-held and laptop computers join IWBs in schools replacing older technologies. Newer devices will continue to appear and spread throughout schools, if they can afford them, but no evidence suggests that these information and communication tools will magically create better teaching and learning.

The Solution, in Our View

Improving classroom teaching and learning requires far more than a technical solution. In those unusual places where technology truly enhances teaching and learning, districts have developed strategic plans for using technology in classroom instruction and invested significant dollars in teacher professional development. Consider Union City, New Jersey, a largely minority and working-class district that has improved students academic achievement over nearly two decades by focusing on prekindergarten, curriculum standards, professional development, and the judicious use of computers in schools.[12]

Information and communication tools can surely help teachers and students do the hard work of teaching and learning, but they cannot replace the all-important connection between teacher, student, and content. The vast resources of the Internet and thousands of software products are of no help to teachers without time and help in figuring out what fits a particular lesson for a particular group of students. If teachers have few opportunities to learn how to use the technology in ways likely to benefit students, the technology will be more hassle than help. Knowing that electronic devices cannot transform teaching and learning in schools, then, is an important first step in returning the central focus to teachers and students rather than technology.

With investments in teaching teachers, the potential for technology to add value grows, provided the technology is easy to use in the classroom and is in working order. Technology can enhance teaching and learning only if the teacher sees the connection to the lesson, knows what to do with it, and decides it is better for students than the existing lesson.

21

Data-Driven Instruction

"EXCUSE ME, WHAT is a data?" asked a teacher at a conference a few years ago.[1] It was a question more powerful than she knew, but not one that she would ask today.

Walk into an elementary school now and you are likely to see a data wall—a section of a wall in a classroom or the teachers' lounge filled with brightly colored cards and charts representing progress for each student. The cards display results on one or more tests, color coded to show different levels of proficiency. The idea is to array data in ways that point to patterns suggesting which students need more help.

Sit in on a grade-level team of teachers and you might see teachers poring over Friday's math test results trying to figure out how to help their students score higher the next time around. More and more, teachers can scan student answer sheets and quickly get a printout list of how each student did on every item along with summary statistics based on tests tied to a particular textbook, teacher-made quiz, or district interim assessment.

Data are everywhere. Data walls, data teams, data cultures—all in the name of improving instruction by looking at student results. No more flying blind, say proponents of data use. Data can now drive instruction. But does widespread access to data improve teaching and learning? What kinds of data are useful to teachers? What does it take to make sense of data and translate it into better teaching?

Where Did the Idea Originate?

The idea that teachers solicit feedback from students to adjust their instruction is as old as teaching. From questions in class to weekly tests to homework, teachers receive a constant flow of information about each student's performance. The idea that numerical data derived from test items are the primary source of information for making instructional decisions is much more recent.

Data-driven instruction has recent ancestors in systems such as mastery learning and curriculum-based assessment, which divide curriculum content into small easy-to-measure components so that each student's progress can be tracked closely. Students move on only when they have demonstrated mastery, often after passing a test.

The more immediate origin of data-driven instruction is the test-based accountability system under NCLB. Coupled with data systems that allow teachers to get immediate results, even on teacher-made tests, timely access to data is no longer a problem in many schools. This is the foreground.

In the background, the increasing influence of businesslike practices to increase efficiency and effectiveness since the 1980s permeates many current reform ideas on how best to improve instruction, including data-driven instruction. Former U. S. Secretary of Education Margaret Spellings was fond of saying, "In God we trust; all others must bring data," a phrase borrowed from business management guru W. Edwards Deming.[2] Whether intended or not, the press for data-driven instruction from policymakers has undercut confidence in teachers' professional judgment.

What Problem Is Data-Driven Instruction Intended to Solve?

Reformers who push for data-driven instruction believe that more reliance on hard numbers will result in better instruction, increased student learning, and higher achievement test scores. The underlying belief among proponents of data-driven instruction is that teachers are too reliant on informal observation, guesswork, and intuition about what students do and do not understand. If presented with hard objective datalike scores on test items, teachers can make more informed decisions about what is and is not working in their classrooms. The more fine-grained the data, the logic goes, the more helpful it becomes. Thus, data from frequent testing that show which students got which questions right, which wrong answers were most frequent, and so on become a gold mine of information for teachers.

With penalties for school staffs that fail to continuously increase student performance on annual state tests, the drive to figure out ways to raise test scores is strong. Data-driven instruction aims to increase teacher effectiveness and student achievement by providing a constant flow of results that can pinpoint the skills each student has and has not learned. Ideally, this information would translate into improved lessons that increase the proportion of students who learn the desired objectives.

Does Data-Driven Instruction Work?

When data-driven instruction is carried out with surgical efficiency, it can have the desired effect of increasing state test scores.[3] Here's roughly how it works. Educators analyze released state test items and determine over the years which state standards have the most questions on the test. This subset of standards, often referred to as power or essential standards, are then scrutinized so that curriculum materials and pacing match the concepts and skills in most heavily tested standards. The next step is district development of interim (usually quarterly) assessments, or benchmarks, that are designed to measure these standards and predict performance on the state test. These then become guides for teachers to devise their own tests that match different parts of the interim assessments. Finally, a few weeks before the state test, teachers take class time to review those topics needing the most attention as judged by interim assessment scores and to focus on those students most likely to move from one proficiency category to the next, the bubble students.

But here's the rub. Do increases in test scores that result from increasingly fine-tuned focus on test items reflect the kind of learning that prepares students for college and careers? Perhaps not. Testing experts point to two serious problems with this approach: a narrowed curriculum and inflated scores. Annual state standardized tests cannot even begin to test all the skills and concepts encompassed by the state's standards. As educators get better and better at figuring out which skills are most likely to show up on the test and focus on these, others get dropped, including entire subject areas as well as hard-to-test concepts. Not only does this result in a lopsided curriculum, it also leads to inflated scores—increases in scores that are much larger than actual increases in student learning.[4] An analysis of New York's math test from 2006 to 2009 provides a clear example of this phenomenon. Half the multiple-choice items on the 2009 test had appeared before in nearly identical form. Altogether, the items covered only a fraction of the skills students were expected to learn each year.[5]

Yet focusing on test items is a rational response given current federal and state high-stakes accountability rules. As a starting point, such a focus can be a positive force. Evidence from students—whether test scores, student work, or teacher observations—gives reason for teachers to collaborate, providing opportunities to figure out what the data mean and implications for instruction.[6] Researchers find, however, that the most overlooked yet most important aspect of data-driven instruction is knowing what action to take given what the data say.[7] Reteaching skills to students who lack them is certainly a benefit. But having a system in place that lets teachers match instruction tailored to each student's needs is a rarity. Studies of effective uses of data that lead to improved student achievement point to the magnitude of the challenge for creating conditions that support wise uses of data and subsequent actions on a broad scale.[8]

The Solution, in Our View

No one can fault the fundamental idea of teachers' basing instructional decisions on systematic collection and analysis of student data. The essence of good teaching starts with understanding what students do and do not understand and knowing what to do when students do not understand. The challenge lies in teachers' knowing which kinds of data—or, more broadly, evidence—are truly informative about what students do and do not know and in their being able to act quickly on what the evidence suggests is needed.

Pinpointing student weaknesses requires casting a net much wider than test scores. All the work that students do during class, from writing to answering questions, provide insights into their learning. Assessments that are truly diagnostic provide information both to teachers and students and contribute to learning.[9] Sometimes called assessments *for* learning rather than assessments *of* learning, such tests are designed by a very different set of principles than traditional multiple-choice tests. They might be paper-and-pencil tests, or they might also be traditional oral questions during class time.

Learning how to design such assessments and ask probing questions that uncover student understanding is no small task. Moreover, doing this systematically and at the proper time is even harder. Teachers can readily learn some simple yet powerful techniques to ensure they have an accurate sense of where all their students stand during a lesson, such as calling on students randomly to answer a question or having the entire class hold up small boards with written responses. Helping teachers get better at asking good questions of students is more likely to have a long-term payoff in student learning than a single-minded focus on what will be on the test. Rather than disparaging teachers' professional judgment, it's a way of strengthening such judgment.

Data-informed instruction doesn't have quite the same sizzle to a politician's ear as *data-driven instruction,* but it points to a more promising way to track student progress than sole reliance on test scores

22

Real-World Learning

STUDENTS FROM LOW-INCOME families are ten times more likely to drop out of high school than those from higher-income families.[1] Could hands-on, real-world experiences change the equation for students who leave high school before graduation?

The emphasis on getting students ready for college in the past decade has driven vocational and career curricula out of most high schools. With a history of tracking and little academic rigor, the focus on a traditional college prep curriculum aims to replace watered-down courses with academic rigor. What's lost are hands-on, real-world activities that can engage students most likely to drop out of high school. The result has been a steady loss in those students who find themselves alienated from traditional academic courses.

Recently, however, new options in curricula called multiple pathways are trying to fill that void.[2] These approaches offer new high school curricula designed around real-world experiences in daily school lessons and workplace settings. The idea is that learning through projects designed around actual problems, will push students to think, collaborate, and learn new content where traditional teacher-directed lessons often fail. Advocates hope that such pathways will increase students' engagement in learning and consequently increase the likelihood that they will stay in school, graduate, and be ready to continue their education or enter the workforce with sufficient skills to satisfy employers.

These new approaches to high school curricula differ not in rigor but in stressing a theme or career focus (e.g., technology occupations, health careers, hotel and restaurant management). They also differ in how courses are organized, in how much time students spend in school, in links with colleges, and in opportunities to work in business and industry. These choices are called by different names: career academies, career/technical education, magnet schools, small learning communities, or off-campus learning.

What they share is an emphasis on learning grounded in real-world problems and situations, what is sometimes called project-based learning. Such projects, when done well, create opportunities for groups of students to investigate meaningful questions that require them to gather information and think critically. Projects might present a problem to solve (How can we decrease waste in the school cafeteria?); a phenomenon to investigate (How do the chemicals in hair dye act on hair cells?); a model to design (Create a scale model of an ideal high school.); or a decision to make (Should the school board vote to build a new school?). For example, students at State College High School in State College, Pennsylvania, figured out how to turn french fry oil from their high school cafeteria into biodiesel fuel to power school furnaces. In Fredericksburg, Texas, students designed working hybrid rockets to meet a set of curriculum specifications. At Jordan High School in Durham, North Carolina, students studying animal science and biotech research created diets for animals using math skills to balance proportions.[3]

Where Did the Concept of Real-World Learning Originate?

Both career preparation and real-world learning approaches have had a long and rich history. Vocational education began in the late nineteenth century as an option for students uninterested in college and was funded by the federal government as early as World War I. With tracking, however, vocational education became a place where students good with their hands found a home and, later, a dumping ground for anyone uninterested in academic subjects. In the 1970s, career education became the reform of the day and tried to make all courses, including those preparing students for college, vocational ones. By the 1980s, career education had passed through the system like a virus and disappeared.[4]

Today's version of career preparation, sometimes referred to as multiple pathways or career-technical education, has arisen from policymakers' growing awareness that careers in health fields, business, technology, media, and other occupations often require college-level courses and technical preparation in classrooms and workplace internships. There is also growing evidence that the current reform emphasis on college prep for everyone still leaves many students disengaged from school and, in largely poor and minority schools, exiting school before graduation, disturbing policymakers, educators, and parents. Unlike the old vocational education curricular track that had become a dumping ground for low-performing students and a pit stop on the road toward dropping out, multiple pathways includes meeting entrance requirements for a range of postsecondary education options.

Its hallmark is an emphasis on real-world learning, both through project-based learning in the classroom and actual experiences in workplace settings. Connections between what happens in schools and what happens in the adult world daily is tighter and therefore far more engaging than constant academic lessons.

This approach to classroom instruction also goes back to John Dewey, whose Lab School exemplified the idea of project-based learning. With a curriculum built around student-centered projects anchored in real-life activities, students collaborated, went on field trips geared toward their project, and did experiments to answer questions they posed. Project-based learning continues today in K–12 schools such as New Tech High Schools, Expeditionary Learning, and The Met.[5]

What Problem Is Real-World Learning Intended to Solve?

The current press for college for all disregards large numbers of students who still drop out. The goal disregards those students who go directly into the workforce after graduation as well as most graduates who enter but do not finish college (4 in 10 white students and 6 in 10 minority students who enter college do not graduate).[6] If all that high school students have is a college prep curriculum, they are woefully unprepared for the workforce. Employers may value academic knowledge, but they attach far more importance to skills needed to be productive in most occupations: punctuality, reliability, professionalism, communications skills, teamwork, and problem solving.[7]

In driving opportunities for real-world problem solving into the high school curriculum and classroom, champions of multiple pathways see the potential to engage student interest, particularly those who are unmotivated to learn in traditional academic classrooms. If engaged, then these students will have workplace opportunities during high school that will better prepare them for lives in which they will likely change jobs and even careers.

Does Real-World Learning Work?

What about schools that have expanded their offerings to include more real-world curriculum, such as career academies, increased ties to technical education in local community colleges, and similar programs—do they work? Unfortunately, few rigorous research studies have been done on such programs.

One particular study, however, was unusual for two reasons. First, in the early 1990s there were so many applicants to urban high school career academies (small personalized programs enrolling 150–200 students at risk of dropping out with strong links to local employers to provide both career awareness and work-based internships and jobs) that the researchers randomly selected applicants to enroll in the academies. Those who were not selected became the control group. This is rare in the field of education. A second and also uncommon feature of this study is that researchers compiled findings over fifteen years of career academy programs and their graduates. Researchers found that those potential dropout students who graduated from these academies (and over 80 percent did), compared to a similar population of students who did not attend academies, earned higher monthly salaries and were more likely to live independently with children and a partner/

spouse. Of course, one study, even with its uncommon design and findings from over a decade of experience, does not constitute proof, but it is a positive sign for career academies.[8]

Another study looked at mathematics achievement in England.[9] Researchers compared a secondary school using traditional instruction with one using project-based instruction. Students in the project-based learning school outperformed the traditional school students in skills and in conceptual and applied knowledge. In fact, in the project-based school, three times as many students passed the national exam.

Most studies of real-world learning, however, focus not on outcomes but on the challenges of implementing these ideas in classrooms. Projects—whether carried out in classrooms or outside the school—do not fit neatly into traditional class period schedules. They take more time than teacher-centered instruction and raise the perennial question of depth versus breadth. This approach is particularly challenging in the context of test-based accountability where pressure to cover curriculum topics and ensure that students do well on those skills tested drives what teachers do.

Organizing students to work on real-world projects requires management and organizational skills that teachers often lack training and experience in doing. Whether on site or off site, real-world projects usually require teacher experience with and student access to the latest technology to provide simulations or opportunities for Internet research or communication with students dispersed to other locations. The available research, then, is thin in pointing to either positive or negative outcomes of multiple pathways or project-based learning.

The Solution, in Our View

College for every high school graduate is a worthwhile ideal to strive for. Still, the reality is that not all students complete high school. Of those that do, many go directly into the labor market, and for those who attend college, many eventually drop out and enter the world of work. Given this reality, arming students with skills, knowledge, and dispositions that prepare them for the workplace is critical. Multiple pathways that link students to the community and to the workplace through career academies and technical education and paid work can expand options, even for students who choose college. From the Job Corps and the Youth Corp to Talent Development High Schools and the Quantum Opportunities Program, models for such alternatives exist.[10]

But expanded options matter only to the extent that they have rigorous curricula and lessons designed to engage students who may already be disillusioned with school. Project-based learning grounded in real-world experiences and problems can provide such motivation. A student's experience on the job—even selling fast food—can become the basis for tackling math problems and writing assignments. In fact, such projects can be equally motivating and demanding in college prep classes. Tying new concepts to concrete problems that interest students can be a benefit to all students.

23

Bridging Two Worlds—
Response to Intervention

L OOKING BACK FROM the early twenty-first century, it is
hard to believe that before 1975 children with disabilities were
largely excluded from schools. Parents kept them at home or put
them in private and public institutions. In the early twentieth century,
schools did enroll a few disabled children, but they were segregated
from the rest of the students.

Today, approaches such as response to intervention (RTI) reflect a
sea change in how public education views and serves students with
disabilities. RTI represents the latest in a series of federal legislative
actions that seek to bridge the historically separate worlds of special
education and regular education.

RTI aims to reduce the numbers of students labeled *learning disabled* through early identification and intervention by the regular classroom teacher. This contrasts with earlier standard practice, required by
law for all students until 2004, in which the regular classroom teacher
refers students with learning problems to a team of specialists for identification of their specific needs and a plan for meeting them, known
as the individualized education plan (IEP) process. RTI hands the first
steps of this process back to the regular classroom teacher.

The underlying premise is that regular teachers are equipped to differentiate and even individualize their instruction, thus intervening and perhaps preventing the development of more serious problems down the road. And, if their intervention in the classroom is insufficient, they (or a school team) can craft interventions for those students with reading, math, or other academic and behavioral problem within each classroom and then assess which students are improving and which are not.[1]

How RTI is designed and implemented varies among districts and states (a few states, such as Colorado, have adopted RTI for all schools and virtually all states have RTI frameworks), but all share certain elements. Basically, RTI has preschool, kindergarten, and general elementary classroom teachers screening, identifying, and monitoring the progress of those students who are having trouble academically and behaviorally. To date, RTI has focused far more on reading in elementary schools than on subject areas within secondary schools.

Usually portrayed as a pyramid of responses, tier 1, the base, is the classroom teacher screening members of her class to see which students are having difficulties and responding by tailoring instruction to the extent possible in the regular classroom. Perhaps nine kindergarteners continue to have trouble in learning the letters of the alphabet, or a second-grade teacher notes that five students regularly fail to turn in homework.

Tier 2 responses commonly mean that a classroom teacher or team intervenes with these students by creating space in the daily schedule beyond the regular class for reteaching, individual attention, or redeploying students to other teachers to use different instructional strategies, materials, and tasks to help targeted students improve their performance.

Tier 3 interventions look to those individual students who continue to have academic difficulties and provide a more intense and tailored response to each student, including further instruction and assessment. Tier 3 interventions can also lead to determining whether particular students have learning or other disabilities.[2]

Advocates praise RTI as an evidenced-based approach to early diagnosis and intervention, filling the need to begin early in general classes to identify academic and behavioral issues before they grow into serious problems. Critics argue that it places a heavy burden (including added paperwork) on classroom teachers who are not well trained to do the kind of assessments and interventions needed. And, they argue, parents can be left out of the process. Advocates view RTI—which one expert calls the "last, best hope" to make all children literate—as a way to apply what has been learned in teaching reading and in special education to general classroom teachers to help disengaged students learn and achieve before being labeled with a disability.[3] Where RTI has been fully embraced, they argue, it is an effective way of doing business for all students, thus bridging general and special education.

Where Did the Idea of RTI Originate?

RTI is the most recent in a series of federal pushes to integrate special education and regular education since the landmark Education for All Handicapped Children legislation was passed in 1975. Now called the Individual with Disabilities Education Improvement Act (IDEIA), all children, regardless of their condition, are required to attend public schools, and districts must provide services to children with identified disabilities. Moreover, they have to provide such services in the least restrictive setting, which for many students means the regular classroom.

Integrating special and regular education has not been easy. Even after the passage of federal laws and the establishment of processes to identify and serve special education students, frequent struggles between parents and district officials have arisen over the identification of particular disabilities (e.g., learning disabled and autistic) and outsourcing services to private providers (e.g., sending particular disabled students to private schools when public schools lack expertise). These battles have led to court cases and swiftly escalating expenditures on special education.

As of 2007, special education students made up nearly 14 percent of U.S. public school enrollment.[4] The cost of educating special education students, however, is on average nearly twice the amount spent to educate a general student. Although the federal government mandates such services, it funds only a small percent of the costs, so the rest comes out of the regular district budget, paving the way for clashes between general and special education.[5]

As a result of these struggles over the past four decades in identifying, placing, and funding special needs students, many highly touted reforms such as inclusion—incorporating all special needs students into general classes and school activities—have been adopted to bridge the large gap between general and special education. Over time, laws, court decisions, and activist reformers have wanted to shrink the differences by merging general and special education.

With the passage of NCLB and the reauthorization of IDEIA have come mandated curriculum standards, testing, and accountability for both general and special education students. With more and more students with disabilities moving into general classes, and with NCLB regulations reducing the number of exemptions from state tests previously given to special education students, pressures to move special needs students into general classes have risen. "It doesn't matter," Alexa Posny, assistant secretary for Special Education and Rehabilitative Services said, "if the child is disadvantaged, disabled, disengaged, disfranchised . . . It doesn't make any difference what they're labeled. We have promised that all students will acquire the same knowledge and skills and that those students who have trouble gaining that knowledge will have help in doing so."[6]

Since 2004, those pressures to include special needs students in general classes have pushed districts to consider ways of preventing academic and behavioral problems in general classrooms. District officials want their teachers to identify as early as possible students in their classrooms who are having problems. For example, as one fifth-grade Colorado teacher put it, "If math homework is not getting done, is it an academic problem or is it an organizational problem? Is it affecting how the student is performing in math?" Asking those questions begins the process of figuring out ways of solving those problems before they become serious and require parents and staff to consider special education.[7]

The main source of pressure for the new emphasis on early prevention stems from the increase in the number of students identified as learning disabled (LD). Since this special education category became official in the late-1970s, it has grown to be the largest category (42 percent) of special needs students. That leap in numbers of LD students has raised troubling questions about the accuracy of the label and how LD students are diagnosed, especially in largely minority and poor urban and rural schools.[8]

For decades, the traditional way to identify a learning disability was to see if there were discrepancies between student scores on intelligence tests and their achievement, especially in reading. Such gaps triggered a formal process involving teachers, specialists, and parents to determine whether the low-achieving student falls into the category of LD. Yet figuring out whether a gap between an intelligence test score and school achievement came from some physical impairment (e.g., vision), mental retardation, emotional disturbance, or economic or social disadvantage was (and is) nearly impossible. As one top federal official said, "Learning disabilities has become a sociological sponge to wipe up the spills of general education . . . It's where children who weren't taught well go." It comes as no surprise, then, that 80 percent of LD students have reading problems and that higher-than-expected percentages of LD students are African American and Hispanic and ELLs.[9]

NCLB (in which Title 1 funds can be used for RTI) and the 2004 IDIEA law sought to bring together general and special education (and provided 15 percent of funds to be used for general education programs). With large percentages of minority students and ELLs being labeled LD, efforts to prevent reading problems from occurring among general students—"to wipe up the spills"—have led many educators to embrace RTI methods as a way of helping all students, particularly those at risk of academic failure, from being slotted into special education.[10]

What Problem Is RTI Intended to Solve?

Too many students with academic and behavioral issues get ignored in general classes until they get identified as special needs. RTI seeks to intervene early in ways that might help students overcome learning problems, get back on track early, and never reach the point of needing referral to special education.

Because of so much uncertainty over exactly what LD means and how best to assess whether children have that disability, policymakers have pressed for solving these problems preventively in general education. It is in these classrooms where teachers can screen, teach, intervene, and monitor students at risk of failing academically.

Basically, by applying approaches used by special education teachers for individual students or general classrooms, RTI aims to prevent academic failures in the primary grades; reduce numbers of students with reading, math, and other academic problems; and keep students in general education programs. This is the instructional bridge between special and general education.

Does RTI Work?

It is too soon to say. Although reform hype boosts RTI as evidence-based and effective, the work in schools and classrooms has yet to show results that would confirm RTI's effectiveness.[11] Researchers tend to study specific elements of RTI, such as assessment techniques, and therefore cannot draw conclusions about the RTI approach overall. For example, while RTI advocates claim the process as being evidence-based, it is far from clear what protocols for screening, diagnosing, and monitoring progress work best with which students (e.g., ELLs, low-income minorities, middle-class whites) in elementary and secondary schools, in different subject areas, and in rural and urban schools.[12]

It is not surprising that researchers do not take on RTI as a whole, since it can look quite different from state to state, district to district, and school to school—and even across classrooms in the same school. Some schools use a three-tiered pyramid for screening and intervention; other use two or four tiers. Some districts mandate school-site coordinators; others do not. Because RTI models differ, questions of fidelity to a uniform RTI do not make sense.[13]

No studies to date offer compelling evidence that RTI reduces the numbers of students assessed as LD or that it leads to more appropriate interventions for all students. And its application to different subject areas, such as math and science, and to secondary school students is still rare.[14]

However, researchers are beginning to study the conditions under which schools are able to implement RTI well. One synthesis of research found several supporting conditions identified across the studies—conditions that we see associated with almost any successful reform: extensive, ongoing professional development; administrative support at the system and building level; teacher buy-in and willingness to adjust their traditional instructional roles; involvement of all school personnel; and adequate meeting time for coordination.[15]

Finally, the question of whether RTI works raises another question—compared to what? Because most students identified as LD end up in the regular classroom, at some point researchers will need to compare the relative effectiveness of RTI and the system it is designed to replace. Because of these problems, the question of whether RTI works remains unanswered.[16]

The Solution, in Our View

RTI focuses on the general classroom and asks teachers to individualize their teaching to meet the varied needs of all students and recommend additional interventions if needed. This is a mammoth undertaking. While many teachers do these tasks regularly, many others lack the expertise and support to systematically diagnose, identify, and assess each of their students across multiple subjects and skills. If RTI is to succeed, teachers need preparation.

Because RTI presumes cooperation among staff—general and special education—to define and mount a range of interventions, schools need to create a climate where staff collaboration and shared responsibility for all students—treating students as *ours* rather than *mine*—can develop. When essential conditions are in place, then the chances of RTI working increase.

RTI seeks to bridge the differences between general and special education by early intervention to prevent emerging academic difficulties from festering into long-term learning deficits that would need special treatment in later years. That idea is noble and worth pursuing as long as districts eager to implement RTI concentrate on building teacher capacities and workplace conditions.

179

Conclusion

What Can Reform-Minded Citizens and Policymakers Do?

EFORMERS CARE DEEPLY about making public schools better, especially for students at risk of failure. Whether they work
in the federal government, state capitals, foundations, universities, corporations, teacher unions, school boards, or local government,
all believe better schools are critical to offering students more promising futures. The problems reformers tackle are real, complex, and
tough to solve. The ideas they promote are often good ones and their
intentions worthy. Yet reform policies too often go awry as they wend
their way into schools and classrooms. The gap between policy and
practice remains vast.

So, what can be done to help policymakers and informed citizens
turn good school reform ideas into sound policies with a real shot at
success? Based on our analysis of twenty-three different reforms, we
have distilled a set of guidelines we believe will assist citizens and educators as well as policymakers from Congress to school boards. Some
of the rules apply more to those who produce reform ideas and policies

(policymakers, advocates, and increasingly foundations); others are more relevant to those who consume them (educators and parents).

Our advice is organized under the three key questions we raised in the introduction to this book: Does a reform make sense? Can the reform actually work in classrooms? Are the conditions for success in place?

Does the Reform Make Sense?

This means looking beyond the hype to the underlying logic and assumptions that connect a reform to the promised results, usually increases in achievement test scores. How does one go about this?

Don't swallow the hype. All claims about reforms overpromise. Elected and appointed policymakers alike exploit criticisms of public education. To gin up support for reforms, they overstate problems: the schools are failing, we rank far behind other countries, teachers are unqualified. And they exaggerate claims: no child will be left behind, competition through choice is the panacea, all students will reach high standards. Reforms are cloaked in the language of *research-based, evidence-based,* and *best practices,* whether or not a shred of evidence exists in support of the idea. In an era of high-stakes testing, proposed reforms guarantee increased test scores with or without any track record of success.

Programs peddled as miracle cures nearly always fail to deliver desired results and therefore disappoint. Disappointment breeds cynicism and helplessness. Policymakers and advocates need to shrink their overpromising on what reforms can deliver and lower the volume of attacks on what is wrong with our public schools. At the same time, educators and citizens need to be skeptical of the hype and press for more truth in advertising about what it takes for a proposed reform to succeed.

Kick the tires. Do the logic and assumptions of the reform hold up? Reforms aim to increase student achievement, yet most are many steps removed from the classroom. More time in school, ending social promotion, and performance pay plans, for example, are all promoted as ways to improve teaching and learning, but the path from each to better teaching and higher test scores is far from clear.

For example, the federal No Child Left Behind Act allows for states to remove the superintendent and school board, and take over a district in which many schools have failed repeatedly to improve academically. The unstated assumption is that there is a cadre of highly trained people who can step in, shape up the central office administration, and somehow transform schools in ways that raise test scores and increase high school graduation rates. However, these people do not exist. If they did, one would hope the state would have dispatched them before year after year of district failure.

Policymakers assume cause-and-effect links between reforms and promised results that rarely exist. Most current reform policies rest on the same chain of logic: educators will put policies into practice that will lead to better curriculum and better teaching, test scores will rise and the gap will narrow, more students will go to college and, as a result, get better jobs. Standards, accountability, charter schools, small high schools—all are expected to improve teaching and learning so scores will rise and students' futures will be rosier. But, in reality, the links between these pieces are not very strong.

The figure titled "Implied Chain of Logic of School Reforms" represents this presumed chain of logic. At the front end, the first arrow on the left suggests that a reform will change what happens in classrooms. The belief that any reform—say, high-stakes testing or small high schools—will lead to better teaching in the absence of a host of other supporting conditions represents the first weak link. This assumption falls into the "and then a miracle happens" school of policy making.[1] Teachers can do more or less of what they already do, but they cannot start doing something they do not know. If sixth-grade teachers don't have any way of learning what probability is and how to teach probability, for example, and if they don't have adequate resources such as a strong curriculum and materials for their students, their teaching is unlikely to change even if test scores are low and penalties are lurking around the corner.

Similarly, the links in the middle of the chain of logic in this figure are tenuous. The connection between better teaching and learning

Implied Chain of Logic of School Reforms

Reforms → Better teaching and learning → Higher test scores / Smaller achievement gap / Higher graduation rates → College → Better jobs

and higher test scores, smaller achievement gaps, and higher graduation rates is weak without other elements, including tests that measure more of what matters and efforts to help students stay in school. The link from these outcomes to college is also weak, assuming much about students' preparation, access to, and resources for college.

Federal, state, and district policymakers and reform advocates can—and should—provide solid arguments and evidence linking their proposals to promised outcomes. The public must press policymakers to state clearly the assumptions underlying the reform and steps needed to achieve the expected result.

Avoid funnel vision. The chain of logic represented above narrows the picture for the future of students. Fixating on test scores as the only accepted measure of learning is the first narrowing of the funnel, much like looking through a keyhole and seeing only part of what's going on in a room. At the end of the chain, the funnel narrows even more, pointing to only one of several desirable outcomes of schooling: better-paying jobs. Other historic goals that the public schools have served for decades, such as civic engagement, building community, and molding character, disappear in the narrow focus on economic success.

This singular focus on academic standards as measured solely by standardized test scores and high-paying jobs seems to have become an article of unquestioned faith held by rich and poor, minority and white, parents and citizens, policymakers and practitioners. Not only is the focus on economic success a narrow one, it ignores labor market realities. Consider that unemployed older adults are taking jobs that high school graduates used to take and that college graduates are facing competition from lower-paid college graduates working remotely in India and other distant locations. And having academic skills is not the end-all of schooling. Employers want graduates who are punctual, reliable, and can talk easily with customers and who are motivated enough to teach themselves by reading a manual.[2] Moreover, the sole focus on college graduation as a stepping-stone to better-paying jobs ignores the many students whose chances of staying on that path are small.

Policymakers can support investment in better tests that look at a broader range of what students can do and avoid policies that rely on single measures. Taxpayers, too, can insist on more than one test and can raise questions about what job opportunities really exist and how students can learn the values and social skills that employers seek.

Can the Reform Actually Work in Classrooms?

Readers should wonder whether reforms require teachers and students to change in ways that are possible. For instance, does the reform connect to what happens in classrooms? Is the reform built on what we know about implementing new programs? Does the reform presume that one size fits all and that all teachers will put in place new programs, no matter what they are?

Where's the beef? For reforms to result in higher student achievement, changes must occur in classrooms. What happens between teachers and students *is* the "beef" of school reform. Simply mandating a new curriculum, however, does not automatically result in teachers changing what they do. And for good reason. Researchers have found that teachers are already making hundreds of decisions a day, motivating and responding to individual students, answering questions, grading papers, and performing dozens of other tasks related to their classes. In addition, teachers know that parents and principals expect them to maintain order, teach the required content and skills, model moral character, and transmit the community's core values. Moreover, these expectations apply to students who are not there by choice, making teachers' jobs that much more demanding.

Any reform aimed at improving student learning depends wholly on how much teachers understand the reform, believe that it will help students learn more and better, and can tailor the reform to their classrooms. If the teacher's perspective is ignored, reforms are less likely to be embraced where it matters the most. Involving experienced educators in designing and choosing reforms increases the likelihood that the reforms will be put into action. Policymakers can invite representative educators to play this role, and taxpayers should insist that they do so.

It's not what you do but how you do it. Policymakers neither run schools nor teach students; they make policy for both from afar. Whether the policy is a new program or a new way of operating, the ideas are only as good as the principals and teachers who put them into practice. In fact, it turns out that how well a program is implemented can matter more than what the program is. A famous evaluation, called the Follow Through Planned Variation experiment, tested a number of different early elementary programs by getting several schools across the country to try each one. One of the key findings, too often ignored today, was that the differences in results from one school to the next *using the same program* were bigger than differences in results between the programs being compared.[3]

Certainly, some programs are better or worse than others. Assuming that a concept has some merit, however, its specifics are often less important than what individual teachers do with it. At one extreme, teachers can ignore a program, which they may do if it does not make sense to them. At the other extreme, teachers can be excited enough by a program to put extra energy and resources into tailoring it to fit their students. Investments in good professional development can increase the likelihood that teachers will give the program a good try.

School context and individual commitment matter greatly. Rather than simply *adopting* a reform, studies have established clearly and unequivocally that both teachers and principals *adapt* reforms continuously to fit their schools and classrooms.[4] The more a reform makes sense to teachers and principals and fits their particular situation, the more likely they are to implement new practices consistent with policy-makers' intent.

Policymakers can acknowledge these lessons from the past and understand what it will take to implement reforms as intended. Educators can help identify what is needed to make reforms work. The result should be policies that provide an appropriate mix of incentives, guidance, and help that leaves room for differences from one place to the next and one person to the next.

One size cannot fit all. One trap that snares all kinds of reforms is that no single solution—one curriculum, one kind of instruction, one particular program—will fit all students and teachers everywhere. What appeals to policymakers looking for efficiencies is that a uniform program appears easier to administer and control—and is often less expensive—than tailoring programs to diverse contexts.

It should be no surprise that many differences exist among states, districts, schools, teachers, and students, given the nation's fifty states and nearly fifteen thousand school districts with over ninety thousand public schools and more than three million teachers instructing more than fifty million students. From differences in neighborhood wealth and community culture to variations in student backgrounds and teacher knowledge, these differences in local context have a huge impact on whether a reform is embraced, how it is carried out, and whether it succeeds. What works well in one school or district is not guaranteed to work in another.

Teachers and principals repeatedly explain that what really matters are the particular children they have in their schools and classrooms. Researchers who have studied reforms know that the particular skills, knowledge, and beliefs of teachers and their bosses also matter in whether and how a reform is put into practice. So, for example, a policy that mandates a highly structured reading program or a K–8 organization may fit some settings but not others. To succeed, policies must be adaptable and flexible.

Reject extremes. Education reform has long been characterized as a pendulum incapable of stopping in the middle. For decades, debates over teaching reading (phonics versus whole language), math (computation versus concepts) and writing (grammar versus content) have polarized policymakers, practitioners, and parents. It may come as a surprise, then, to learn that these wars are fought largely in speeches, articles, and conferences, not in actual classroom practices. More often than not, research shows, teachers reject extremist positions and find the best solution to be a balance between polar opposites.[5]

Similarly, extreme positions are staked out around scripted curriculum and teacher-invented curriculum. At one extreme, advocates assume that teachers are unable to exercise any judgment and therefore need textbooks that specify word-for-word what they should say to their students. At the other extreme, teachers are viewed as creative inventors who can design their own curricula with minimal tools and materials. Most educators reject both extremes, yet they find little support for the middle ground from textbook publishers and district leaders.

Policies that insist on extreme positions invite resistance. To increase the likelihood that programs will lead to desired results, policymakers and the public must seek a middle ground. One such option is to provide choices in reading programs, for example, or provide flexibility to educators to adapt approaches to their circumstances.

Déjà vu all over again. No wonder the distilled wisdom that teachers and principals offer newcomers to school reform is, "stay in one place long enough and the same reform returns like a bad penny." Time and again, policies that promote curricular change or rely on tests to determine students' futures have been tried, yet few policymakers ever looked in the rearview mirror for help in shaping policies. Only with evidence about why policies did or did not work out as intended will reformers be spared predictable failures. Evaluations of earlier reforms don't provide ready answers to today's questions, but they do provide considerable guidance on what it takes to increase a reform's likelihood of success. Policymakers and citizens can ask more questions about what happened when similar reforms were tried in the past.

Don't throw out the baby with the bathwater. Policies can at best be only hunches about what will work in schools, and even the best guesses, grounded in all available evidence, are no guarantee of success. Policymakers and citizens need to keep an eye on what happens to reforms and an ear out for the reactions of teachers and students. Negative reactions and problems are not necessarily signs that a reform should be abandoned, but they likely point to needed adjustments. Figuring out the right adjustments may require more systematic information gathering. Neither abandoning a reform prematurely nor steadfastly sticking with something that isn't working, even if it is politically popular, will contribute to improving schools.

Treating reform policies as ideas to be improved on or rejected is a sensible (and morally responsible) way of dealing with policies that have important consequences for both adults and children.

Are the Conditions for Success in Place?

School reforms contain assumptions about what teachers and administrators already know how to do and what it will take for them to carry out the reforms, but are they accurate? Whether administrators and teachers change what they do to conform to a new reform policy depends on a host of factors, many beyond the control of policymakers. But one factor is under their control: providing the resources to ensure that educators understand and know how to do what they are being asked to do.

Ready or not. Policymakers are typically too far removed from the classroom to fully appreciate what teachers and principals need to have in place to make reforms work. In the absence of discussions with educators, school reform policies are likely to ignore the minimal conditions and resources needed for a reform to have a chance of success. For example, many reforms assume that teachers and administrators have what they need to do a better job, including not only the know-how but also the necessary materials, help, and professional development. In fact, the conditions present in the poorest and lowest-performing schools are often the opposite of what is needed for improvement. Without dealing directly with issues of distrust and racism, as well as poor training and other needs, efforts to change instruction will fall flat.

Citizens must call attention to the real conditions for teaching and learning in their schools and ensure that policymakers hear directly from educators.

No cheap fix. Too many reforms are promoted as if school improvement aimed at higher academic achievement can be done for pennies. Creating the conditions for success requires far more than grabbing innovations. For example, as we have shown, reforms cannot succeed without well-trained teachers. This will mean hiring tens of thousands of such teachers and providing opportunities for continuous learning to those already in the classroom. If the professional development is of a high caliber, it will require an investment of teachers' time in learning communities plus coaching or mentoring as teachers learn new approaches. So the costs for increasing the number of highly skilled people must be included.

Yet policymakers predictably choose to spend millions of dollars on new tests that every child must take rather than the billions it would cost to raise teacher salaries, to attract and keep qualified teachers, and to retrain current teachers. This happens even though a 2005 Education Testing Service public opinion poll showed that 80 percent of Americans agree that teacher salaries should be increased even if it means raising taxes.[6]

This quest for cheap fixes becomes especially evident in the persistent failure of low-income, largely minority urban and rural schools. So many reforms presume that schools alone are responsible for catastrophic dropout rates, unyielding achievement gaps, and high turnover among school leaders and staffs. Thus, policymakers act as though standards-based curriculum, testing, and accountability measures will remedy these severe problems while failing to provide the resources teachers need and the support necessary beyond the schools, from health services to retraining programs for the unemployed. Insufficient resources will doom the best of reform ideas. Although money is no guarantee of success, lack of money predictably leads to failure.

Additional costs arise from the unexpected consequences of reform policies. Under California's class size reduction policy, for example, two major costs were unanticipated: the dollar cost for additional classroom space for every school in the state and the cost of lower teacher quality in the state's poorest schools. Reducing class size in kindergarten through third grade meant that every elementary school needed to hire new teachers right away. This resulted in hiring tens of thousands of uncertified teachers, most of whom ended up teaching in the poorest schools.[7]

Other costs are quite predictable. Unlike prescription drugs, however, the possible negative side effects of reform policies are rarely mentioned, which means they cannot be weighed against possible benefits. For example, holding third graders back based on a single test score could contribute to future failure and dropout rates. Similarly, denying diplomas to students who fail to pass a graduation test means that some students, mostly minority, will leave school without the credential considered essential for even an entry-level job.

Policymakers and citizens alike need to be aware of the real costs of underwriting major reform efforts. If the necessary money is not forthcoming, policymakers and the public should adjust their expectations accordingly. It makes no sense to assume that lofty goals can be achieved regardless of whether the needed resources are in place.

An Ounce of Prevention. Waiting until students reach kindergarten to begin to close the achievement gap makes both the challenge and the costs extraordinary. For school reforms to succeed, reforms directed to gaps in learning at a much earlier age are essential. In fact, prenatal care is the starting point for many later learning problems. It is indisputable that gaps in achievement are closely related to income: poor children start school significantly behind their more affluent peers. Attention to gaps, most of which can be traced to poverty, means attention to known problems before children reach school age.

Although such investments would be enormously expensive, continued inattention is even more expensive. High dropout rates for poor and minority students exact huge costs on society. Those who drop out are far more likely to end up unemployed and in jail, both of which cost society considerably more than public schooling.[8] If the goals of school reform are to be realized, it's going to mean reaching beyond the bounds of school reform policies.

These guidelines may help readers make sense of school reforms, to cut through the hype to see both the promise and the pitfalls. Simple answers and hoped-for miracles don't make a dent in the real world of schools and classrooms, except to fan disillusionment. We believe we have posed questions worth asking of any reform and offered lessons about the journey from policy to practice.

The good ideas underlying the reforms reviewed here, and many others not included, deserve nurturing. But it's important to remember that the benefits of change can easily get lost in the translation from good ideas into policies and from policies into classroom practice.

Reformers and policymakers of all stripes must try to understand what motivates and helps teachers and students to do more and what does not, especially in the nation's most challenging classrooms. The more they understand, the more likely it is that their ideas and the policies based on those ideas will reach the target and show results.

If policymakers and citizens adjust their expectations for reform to reflect the investments, their disappointments will diminish. If those who champion good ideas keep their eyes on the classroom, they can keep school reforms on track.

Notes

Chapter 1

1. George H. W. Bush, "Remarks at the University of Virginia Convocation," September 28, 1980, http://www.presidency.ucsb.edu/ws/index.php?pid=17578.

2. The most prominent of these is *A Nation at Risk: The Imperative for Educational Reform* (Washington, DC: National Commission on Excellence in Education, 1983), http://www2.ed.gov/pubs/NatAtRisk/index.html.

3. Quoted in Governor Gary Locke's "State of Education Address," October 19, 1999, http://www.digitalarchives.wa.gov/governorlocke/speeches/speech-view. asp?SpeechSeq=172.

4. Barack Obama, "Remarks to the Hispanic Chamber of Commerce on a Complete and Competitive American Education," March 10, 2009, http://www. whitehouse.gov/the_press_office/Remarks-of-the-President-to-the-United-States-Hispanic-Chamber-of-Commerce/.

5. Naomi Chudowsky, Victor Chudowsky, and Nancy Kober, *Are Achievement Gaps Closing and Is Achievement Rising for All?* (Washington, DC: Center on Education Policy, 2009).

6. Anna Habash Rowan, Daria Hall, and Kati Haycock, *Gauging the Gaps: A Deeper Look at Student Achievement* (Washington, DC: Education Trust, 2010).

7. Lynn Olson, "A Proficient Score Depends on Geography," *Education Week*, February 2, 2002, http://www.edweek.org/ew/articles/2002/02/20/23proficie nt.h21.html?qs=Lynn+Olson.

8. Pat Kossan, Anne Ryman, and Ryan Konig, "More Kids Pass '05 AIMS," *Arizona Republic,* July 13, 2005, http://www.azcentral.com/families/education/ articles/0713aims13.html.

9. Debra Viadero, "NCES Finds States Lowered 'Proficiency' Bar," *Education Week*, October 29, 2009, http://www.edweek.org/ew/articles/2009/10/29/10nces. h29.html?qs=States+lowered+proficiency.

10. Marguerite Roza and Paul T. Hill, "How Within-District Spending Inequities Help Some Schools Fail," and Kati Haycock, "The Elephant in the Living Room," both in *Brookings Papers on Education Policy: 2004,* ed. Diane Ravitch (Washington, DC: Brookings Institution Press, 2004).

Chapter 2

1. "News from the Committee on Education and the Workforce," press release, Rep. John Boehner, chairman, February 11, 2003, http://webcache.googleusercontent.com/search?q=cache:haRVTYOhJxcJ:republicans.edlabor.house.gov/archive/press/press108/02feb/newreport021103.htm.

2. W. James Popham, "Why Standardized Tests Don't Measure Educational Quality," *Educational Leadership* 6 (March 1999): 8–14.

3. Erik W. Robelen, "State Reports on Progress Vary Widely," *Education Week,* September 3, 2003.

4. *The Accountability Illusion* (Washington, DC: The Thomas B. Fordham Institute, 2009).

5. Dan Hardy, "Rule Changes Aided School Progress," *Philadelphia Inquirer,* October 28, 2004, A1.

6. In late 2005, the U.S. Department of Education announced waivers for a few states to measure progress instead of simply reporting whether the standard was reached.

7. For a clear, detailed explanation on this and other limitations of testing, see Daniel Koretz, *Measuring Up: What Educational Testing Really Tells Us* (Cambridge, MA; Harvard University Press, 2008).

8. See, for example, Wayne Au, "High-stakes Testing and Curricular Control: A Qualitative Metasynthesis," *Educational Researcher* 36, no. 5 (2007): 258–267; Laura S. Hamilton, Brian M. Stecher, Jennifer Lin Russell, Julie A. Marsh, and Jeremy Miles, "Accountability and Teaching Practices: School-level Actions and Teacher Responses," in *Strong States, Weak Schools: The Benefits and Dilemmas of Centralized Accountability,* ed. Bruce Fuller, Melissa Henne, and Emily Hannum (Bingley, UK: JAI Press, 2008), 31–66.

9. Lorraine M. McDonnell and Craig Choisser, *Testing and Teaching: Local Implementation of New State Assessments,* CSE Technical Report 442 (Los Angeles: National Center for Research on Evaluation, Standards, and Student Testing [CRESST], 1997); Daniel Koretz, Karen Mitchell, Sheila Baron, and Sarah Keith, *Final Report: Perceived Effects of the Maryland School Performance Assessment Program,* CSE Technical Report 409 (Los Angeles: CRESST, 1996).

10. Bobby D. Rampey, Gloria S. Dion, and Patricia L. Donahue, *The Nation's Report Card: Trends in Academic Progress in Reading and Mathematics 2008* (Washington, DC: U.S. Department of Education, 2009); Sean Cavanagh, "NAEP Math Scores Idle at 4th Grade, Advance at 8th," *Education Week,* October 14, 2009, http://www.edweek.org/ew/articles/2009/10/14/08naep.h29.html?qs=NAEP+Math+Scores+Idle+at+4th+Grade,+Advance+at+8th.

11. Interviewed by Jane David in 2002 as part of a study that promised anonymity to respondents.

12. Joshua Benton and Holly K. Hacker, "Poor Schools' TAKS Surges Raise Cheating Questions," *Dallas Morning News,* December 30, 2004, http://www.dallasnews.com/sharedcontent/dws/dn/education/stories/121904dnmetcheating.64fa3.html.

13. Lawrence A. Uzzell, *No Child Left Behind: The Dangers of Centralized Education Policy*, Policy Analysis Report No. 544 (Washington, DC: Cato Institute, 2005), 15.

14. Heinrich Mintrop and Tina Trujillo, *Corrective Action in Low-Performing Schools: Lessons for NCLB Implementation from State and District Strategies in First-Generation Accountability Systems*, CSE Report 641 (Los Angeles: CRESST, 2004).

Chapter 3

1. "Income, Poverty, and Health Insurance Coverage in the United States: 2003," in *Current Population Reports*, prep. Carmen DeNavas-Walt, Bernadette D. Proctor, and Robert J. Mills (Washington, DC: U.S. Census Bureau, 2004).

2. Marguerite Roza and Sarah Yatsko, *Beyond Teacher Reassignments: Better Ways Districts Can Remedy Salary Inequities Across Schools* (Seattle: University of Washington, 2010).

3. Kati Haycock and Karin Chenoweth, "Choosing to Make a Difference," *American School Board Journal* n.v. (April 2005): 28.

4. Bobby D. Rampey, Gloria S. Dion, and Patricia L. Donahue, *NAEP 2008 Trends in Academic Progress* (NCES 2009–479), National Center for Education Statistics, 2009, http://nces.ed.gov/nationsreportcard/pubs/main2008/2009479.asp#pdflist.

5. On closer inspection, some researchers have suggested that the narrowing of the racial gaps in Texas was more illusory than real—the result of a limit on how high the top students could score and high dropout rates. National data from 1992 to 1998 suggest an increasing gap over much of the 1990s for Texas and the country in general. NAEP, "The Nation's Report Card Reading Highlights 2003," http://nces.ed.gov/nationsreportcard/reading/results2003/stateracegap-g4.asp.

6. Anna Habash Rowan, Daria Hall, and Kati Haycock, *Gauging the Gaps: A Deeper Look at Student Achievement* (Washington, DC: Education Trust, 2010).

7. Sam Dillon, "'No Child' Law Is Not Closing a Racial Gap," *New York Times*, April 28, 2009, http://www.nytimes.com/2009/04/29/education/29scores.html?_r=1&ref=education.

8. Naomi Chudowsky, Victor Chudowsky, and Nancy Kober, *Are Achievement Gaps Closing and Is Achievement Rising for All?* (Washington, DC: Center on Education Policy, 2009).

9. Lynn Olson, "A 'Proficient' Score Depends on Geography," *Education Week*, February 20, 2002.

10. David J. Hoff, "Texas Judge Rules Funds Not Enough," *Education Week*, September 22, 2004.

11. National Governors Association, "Closing the Achievement Gap," issue brief, May 27, 2003, http://www.subnet.nga.org/educlear/achievement/.

Chapter 4

1. Sam Dillon, "Charter Schools Alter Map of Public Education in Dayton," *New York Times,* March 27, 2005; Terry Ryan, "Charter Schools, City Schools Have to Work Together," *Dayton Daily News*, November 27, 2009, http://www.daytondailynews.com/blogs/content/shared-gen/blogs/dayton/opinion/entries/2009/11/27/guest_column_charter_city_scho.html.

2. Keisha Hegamin, "Real Choice Should Be Available for All," *Philadelphia Public School Notebook,* fall 2003, http://www.thenotebook.org/editions/2003/fall/real.htm.

3. *Pierce v. Society of Sisters* (1925), http://straylight.law.cornell.edu/supct/html/historics/USSC_CR_0268_0510_ZO.html.

4. National Alliance for Public Charter Schools, "Number of Public Charters and Students, 2009–2010," http://www.publiccharters.org/enrollment.

5. For data on EMOs, see the Education and the Public Interest Center Web site, http://epicpolicy.org/newsletter/2009/10/nonprofit-public-school-management-organizations-still-growing.

6. See the U.S. Department of Education Web site devoted to NCLB, http://www.ed.gov/nclb/landing.jhtml?src=pb.

7. Rick Jervis, "High Marks for New Orleans Charter Schools," *USA Today*, August 27, 2009, http://www.usatoday.com/news/nation/2009-08-26-new-orleans-charter-schools_N.htm.

8. David Nagel, "Charter School Support Is a Prerequisite for Race to the Top Funds," *The Journal,* June 9, 2009, http://thejournal.com/articles/2009/06/09/charter-school-support-is-a-prerequisite-for-race-to-the-top-funds.aspx.

9. Jennifer Mrozowski, "Charters Have High Turnover," *Cincinnati Enquirer,* June 30, 2005, A1; Pat Kossan, "New Tests Sought for Arizona Charter Schools," *Arizona Republic*, April 26, 2009, http://www.azcentral.com/arizona-republic/news/articles/2009/04/26/20090426showdown0426.html.

10. Dan Goldhaber, "School Choice: An Examination of the Empirical Evidence on Achievement, Parental Decision Making, and Equity," *Educational Researcher* 28, no. 9 (1999): 16–25; Katrina Bulkley and Jennifer Fisler, *A Decade of Charter Schools: From Theory to Practice,* CPRE Policy Briefs, RB-35 (Philadelphia: Consortium for Policy Research in Education, 2002); Diana Schemo, "Nation's Charter Schools Lagging Behind, U.S. Test Scores Reveal," *New York Times*, August 17, 2004, A21; Michael Dobbs, "Charter Students Fare No Better, Study Says," *Washington Post*, December 16, 2004, A3; Frederick Hess, *Revolution at the Margins* (Washington, DC: Brookings Institution Press, 2002); Nick Anderson, "Charter Schools: Two Studies, Two Conclusions," *Washington Post,* November 30, 2009, B2. See eleven independent evaluations of KIPP programs between 2001 and 2008 at http://www.kipp.org/about-kipp/results/independent-reports.

11. Frederick M. Hess, *Revolution at the Margins: The Impact of Competition on Urban School Systems* (Washington, DC: Brookings Institution Press, 2002); Christopher Lubienski, "Innovation in Education Markets: Theory and Evidence on the Impact of Competition and Choice in Charter Schools," *Ameri-*

can *Educational Research Journal* 40, no. 2 (2003): 395–443; Kevin Booker, Scott M. Gilpatric, Timothy Gronberg, and Dennis Jansen, "The Effect of Charter Schools on Traditional Public School Students in Texas: Are Children Who Stay Behind Left Behind?" *Journal of Urban Economic* 64 (July 2008): 123–145; Yongmei Ni, "The Impact of Charter Schools on the Efficiency of Traditional Public Schools: Evidence from Michigan," *Economics of Education Review* 28 (October 2009): 571–584; Ron Zimmer, Brian Gill, Kevin Booker, Stephane Lavertu, Tim R. Sass, and John Witte, *Charter Schools in Eight States: Effects on Achievement, Attainment, Integration, and Competition* (Santa Monica, CA: RAND, 2009).

12. Education Sector, *Growing Pains: Scaling Up the Nation's Best Charter Schools,* (Washington, DC: Education Sector 2009). See also Deborah Viadero, "Study Casts Doubt on Strength of Charter Managers," *Education Week,* December 3, 2009, http://www.edweek.org/ew/collections/eye-on-research/index.html.

13. Charter schools are substantially more segregated by race, wealth, disabling condition, and language than the districts in which they reside, according to one national study. See Gary Miron, Jessica L. Urschel, William J. Mathis, and Elana Tornquist, *Schools Without Diversity: Education Management Organizations, Charter Schools, and the Demographic Stratification of the American School System* (Boulder, CO: Education and the Public Interest Center & Education Policy Research Unit, 2010).

Chapter 5

1. Roger Lowenstein, "The Quality Cure? *New York Times Magazine*, March 13, 2005, 50.

2. Richard Murnane and David Cohen, "Merit Pay and the Evaluation Problem: Why Most Merit Pay Plans Fail and a Few Survive," *Harvard Educational Review* 56, no. 1 (1986): 15.

3. See, for example, U.S. Department of Education, "Teacher Incentive Fund: Program Description," http://www2.ed.gov/programs/teacherincentive/index.html, updated 2010.

4. Crystal Yednak and Katie Fretland, "In Race for U.S. School Grants Is a Fear of Winning," *New York Times*, January 16, 2010; Jason Song, "Districts Refusing Reforms Could Hurt California's Chances for Grant Money," *Los Angeles Times,* February 17, 2010.

5. Diana Schemo, "When Students' Gains Help Teachers' Bottom Line," *New York Times,* May 9, 2004.

6. Steven Greenhouse, "Union Chief Seeks to Overhaul Teacher Evaluation Process," *New York Times,* January 17, 2010, A21.

7. Excerpts from Governor Arnold Schwarzenegger's "State of the State Address," January 6, 2005, http://www.signonsandiego.com/uniontrib/20050106/news_lz1n6excerpts.html.

8. Lauren Smith, "D.C. Schools Chief Michelle Rhee Fights Union Over Teacher Pay," *U.S. News and World Report,* December 21, 2009, http://www.usnews.

com/news/national/articles/2009/12/21/dc-schools-chief-michelle-rhee-fights-union-over-teacher-pay.html.

9. Unlike end-of-year test scores, which do not show how much students learned over the school year, value-added measures are designed to measure progress by taking into account where students were at the end of the previous school year. Such measures also attempt to take into account other factors that influence students' test scores, since scores can be used to judge individual teachers whose students, schools, and communities can be quite different. For example, teachers with students who are absent frequently or who struggle with English or teachers who work in schools with few resources (e.g., not enough textbooks or desks or supplies) would not be expected to gain as much as those who do not face such challenges. Whether or not value-added measures do a good job of sorting out how much progress is due to the teacher is open to debate, leading most testing experts to conclude that such measures should not be the sole basis for decisions that are consequential for individuals.

10. Brendan Rapple, "Payment by Results: An Example of Assessment in Elementary Education in 19th-Century Britain," *Education Policy Analysis Archives* 2, no. 1 (1994), http://epaa.asu.edu/epaa/v2n1.html.

11. Jane G. Coggshall, Amber Ott, and Molly Lasagna, *Retaining Teacher Talent: Convergence and Contradictions in Teachers' Perceptions of Policy Reform Ideas* (Naperville, IL: Learning Point Associates; New York: Public Agenda, 2010), http://www.learningpt.org/expertise/educatorquality/genY/CommunicatingReform/index.php.

12. Ericka Mellon, "HISD Passes Teacher Dismissal Plan," *Houston Chronicle,* February 12, 2010.

13. "2010 Annual Letter from Bill Gates: Helping Teachers Improve," Bill and Melinda Gates Foundation, http://www.gatesfoundation.org/annual-letter/2010/Pages/helping-teachers-improve-education-united-states.aspx.

14. Susan Moore Johnson, Susan M. Kardos, David Kauffman, Edward Liu, and Morgaen L. Donaldson, "The Support Gap: New Teachers' Early Experiences in High-Income and Low-Income Schools," *Education Policy Analysis Archives* 12 (2004), http://epaa.asu.edu/epaa/v12n61.

Chapter 6

1. Debra Viadero, "Big City Mayors' Control of Schools Yields Mixed Results," *Education Week,* September 11, 2000; Geeta Anand, "Menino Pledges Better Schools," *Boston Globe,* January 18, 1996; Donovan Slack and Michael Levenson, "Fifth Term for Menino," *Boston Globe,* November 4, 2009, http://www.boston.com/news/local/massachusetts/articles/2009/11/04/with_turnout_high_mayor_menino_sails_to_unprecedented_victory/; Stephen Witt, "Bloomberg Re-Elected for a Third Term," *New York Post,* November 4, 2009, http://www.nypost.com/p/news/local/brooklyn/item_ujaMWoJKycwgIaoT0beTpI.

2. Michael Usdan, "Boston: The Stars Finally in Alignment," in *Powerful Reforms with Shallow Roots,* ed. Larry Cuban and Michael Usdan (New York: Teachers College Press, 2003), 38–53.

3. Dorothy Shipps, "Updating Tradition: The Institutional Underpinnings of Modern Mayoral Control in Chicago's Public Schools," in *When Mayors Take Charge,* ed. Joseph Viteritti (Washington, DC: Brookings Institution Press, 2009), 136–139; Martha Moore, "More Mayors Move to Take over Schools," *USA Today,* March 22, 2007, http://www.usatoday.com/news/education/2007-03-20-cover-mayors-schools_N.htm.

4. Michael Kirst, *Mayoral Influence, New Regimes, and Public School Governance,* CPRE Research Report No. RR-049 (Philadelphia: Consortium for Policy Research in Education, 2002). For Detroit, see Christine MacDonald and Brad Heath, "Detroit School Reform Falters," *Detroit News,* October 24, 2004, http://www.detnews.com/2004/specialreport/0410/24/a01-312953.htm. One scholar who does make the claim that mayoral control has had a positive effect on academic achievement is Kenneth Wong, "Does Mayoral Control Improve Performance?" in Viteritti, *When Mayors Take Charge,* 64–87. However, in the same book, Jeffrey Henig challenges Wong's conclusions ("Mayoral Control: What We Can and Cannot Learn from Other Cities," 19–45).

5. Elissa Gootman and David Herszenhorn, "Mayor Hails 'New Era' in Schools Amid Crowding Fears," *New York Times*, September 5, 2003, B4.

6. Karla Reid, "Mayors Stepping up to Improve Quality of City Schools," *Education Week,* April 9, 2003.

Chapter 7

1. As stated in the preface, we were both part of the Cardozo Project in Urban Teaching in the 1960s, the forerunner of the Urban Teacher Corps and the National Teacher Corps. For a description of the Cardozo Project in Urban Teaching, see Larry Cuban, *To Make a Difference: Teaching in the Inner City* (New York: Free Press, 1970).

2. Richard Ingersoll, "Teacher Shortage: Myth or Reality," *Education Horizons* 81, no. 3 (2003): 146–152.

3. "Overview of Alternative Routes to Teacher Certification," National Center for Alternative Certification, http://www.teach-now.org/overview.cfm.

4. National Academy of Education, *Teacher Quality: Improving Teacher Quality and Distribution,* Education Policy Briefing Sheet (Washington, DC: National Academy of Education, 2008).

5. National Center for Alternative Certification, http://www.teach-now.org/.

6. Recent news reports suggest that the recession and associated job cutbacks may change this equation. See, for example, James Haug, "Teachers Wary of Recruitment Group," *Las Vegas Review-Journal,* June 7, 2010, B10.

7. *"Teacher Quality" Education Policy White Paper* (Washington, DC: National Academy of Education, 2009).

8. Institute of Educational Sciences, "An Evaluation of Teachers Trained Through Different Routes to Certification," NCEE 2009-4043, February 2009, http://ies.ed.gov/ncee/pubs/20094043/index.asp.

9. Daniel C. Humphrey, Marjorie E. Wechsler, and Heather J. Hough, "Characteristics of Effective Alternative Teacher Certification Programs," *Teachers*

College Record 110, no. 1 (2008): 1–63, http://www.tcrecord.org/Content. asp?ContentId=12613.

10. Kati Haycock and Eric Hanushek, "An Effective Teacher in Every Classroom," *Education Next* 10, no. 3 (2010), http://educationnext.org/an-effective-teacher-in-every-classroom/.

11. See, for example, Morgaen Lindsay Donaldson, "Teach for America Teachers' Careers: Whether, When and Why They Leave Low-Income Schools and the Teaching Profession" (PhD diss., Graduate School of Education, Harvard University, 2008); Thomas J. Kane, Jonah E. Rockoff, and Douglas O. Staiger, "What Does Certification Tell Us About Teacher Effectiveness? Evidence from New York City," Working Paper 12155, National Bureau of Economic Research, Cambridge, MA, April 2006; Donald Boyd, Pamela Grossman, Hamilton Lankford, Susanna Loeb, and James Wyckoff, "How Changes in Entry Requirements Alter the Teacher Workforce and Affect Student Achievement," *Education Finance and Policy* 1, no. 2 (2006): 176–216.

12. *"Teacher Quality" Education Policy White Paper.*

Chapter 8

1. Melissa Roderick, Mimi Engel, and Jenny Nagaoka, *Ending Social Promotion: Results from Summer Bridge* (Chicago: Consortium on Chicago School Research, 2003).

2. "NCES Dropout Rates in the United States: 1995," NCES 97-473, http://nces. ed.gov/pubs/dp95/97473-5.asp; National Research Council, "Promotion and Retention," in *High Stakes: Testing for Tracking, Promotion, and Graduation,* ed. Jay P. Heubert and Robert M. Hauser (Washington, DC: National Academy Press, 1999).

3. Shane E. Jimerson, "A Synthesis of Grade Retention Research: Looking Backward and Moving Forward," *California School Psychologist* 6, no. 1 (2001): 47–59; Jenny Nagaoka and Melissa Roderick, *Ending Social Promotion: The Effects of Retention* (Chicago: Consortium on Chicago School Research, 2004).

4. Pete Goldschmidt, "When Can Schools Affect Dropout Behavior? A Longitudinal Multilevel Analysis," *American Education Research Journal* 36, no. 4 (1999): 715–738.

5. Nagaoka and Roderick, *Ending Social Promotion.*

6. Lorrie S. Shepherd and Mary L. Smith, *Flunking Grades: Research and Policies on Retention* (London: Falmer Press, 1989).

7. Suh-Ruu Ou and Arthur Reynolds, "Grade Retention, Post-Secondary Education, and Public Aid Receipt," *Educational Evaluation and Policy Analysis* 32, no. 1 (2010): 118–139.

Chapter 9

1. Jeffrey Gettleman, "The Segregated Classrooms of a Proudly Diverse School," *New York Times,* April 3, 2005. An updated National Public Radio

program highlighted the continuing conflict over the achievement gap and tracking. See Nancy Solomon, "The Racial Achievement Gap Still Plagues Schools," *NPR,* October 31, 2009, http://www.npr.org/templates/story/story.php?storyId=114298676.

2. James Gallagher, "When Ability Grouping Makes Good Sense," *Education Week*, October 28, 1992, http://www.edweek.org/ew/articles/1992/10/28/08galla.h12.html?querystring=james%20gallagher%20ability%20grouping. The pro and con arguments for tracking are summarized in Joseph Kahne, *Reframing Educational Policy* (New York: Teachers College Press, 1996), 59–68; and Jeannie Oakes, *Keeping Track* (New Haven, CT: Yale University Press, 1985), 15–39.

3. Gettleman, "The Segregated Classrooms of a Proudly Diverse School."

4. For back-and-forth researcher views on tracking, see Oakes, "Keeping Track," 700–712; Kevin Welner, "Non-Evidence About Tracking: Critiquing the New Report from The Fordham Institute," *Teachers College Record,* December 13, 2009, http://www.tcrecord.org/Content.asp?ContentId=15872.

5. Peter Schmidt, "Debate over Ability Grouping Gains High Profile," *Education Week*, October 13, 1993, http://www.edweek.org/ew/articles/1993/10/13/16side.h12.html?querystring=ability%20grouping.

6. Debra Viadero, "On the Wrong Track," *Teacher Magazine*, January 1999, 22–23.

7. Maureen Hallinan, "The Detracking Movement," *Education Next*, Fall 2004, http://www.educationnext.org/20044/72.html; Jeannie Oakes and Amy Wells, "Detracking for High Student Achievement," *Educational Leadership* 55, no. 6, (1998): 38–41.

8. Tom Loveless, "The Tracking and Ability Grouping Debate," The Thomas Fordham Foundation, 2003, http://www.edexcellence.net/foundation/publication/publication.cfm?id=127.

Chapter 10

1. Bill Gates's prepared remarks at the National Education Summit on High Schools, Washington, DC, February 26–27, 2005, http://www.achieve.org/achieve.nsf/2005Summit?OpenForm.

2. National Education Summit on High Schools "Briefing Book," February 2005, http://www.achieve.org/achieve.nsf/StandardForm3?openform&parentunid=B277BD2D98CE9CA485256FEF00711757.

3. Estimates of dropout and graduation rates are hotly debated. A consensus has emerged around 70 percent as the current estimate of graduation rate, but how much lower that is than previously has less agreement. See Christopher B. Swanson and Duncan Chaplin, "Counting High School Graduates when Graduates Count: Measuring Graduation Rates under the High Stakes of NCLB," Urban Institute, February 2003, http://www.urban.org/urlprint.cfm?ID=8299; and Paul Barton, *One-Third of a Nation: Rising Dropout Rates and Declining Opportunities* (Princeton NJ: Educational Testing Service, 2005).

4. National Center for Public Policy and Higher Education, "Policy Alert: The Educational Pipeline: Big Investment, Big Returns," April 2004, http://www.

highereducation.org/reports/pipeline/. Note that these estimates vary depending on definitions of continuing one's education (immediately or within a certain number of years after high school graduation) and the number of years used for defining on-time graduation from college.

5. Jay P. Greene and Marcus A. Winters, *Public High School Graduation and College-Readiness Rates: 1991–2002,* Education Working Paper No. 8. (New York: Manhattan Institute for Policy Research, 2005).

6. Patricia A. Wasley et al., *Small Schools Great Strides: A Study of New Small Schools in Chicago* (New York: Bank Street College of Education, 2000).

7. Erik W. Robelen, "Gates High Schools Get Mixed Review in Study," *Education Week,* November 16, 2005.

8. Sarah Dewees, "The School-within-a-School Model," ERIC Clearinghouse on Rural Education and Small Schools, 1999, ED43847, http://www.ericdigests.org/2000-4/school.htm.

9. Linda Shear et al., "Contrasting Paths to Small-School Reform: Results of a 5-year Evaluation of the Bill and Melinda Gates Foundation's National High Schools Initiative," *Teachers College Record* 110 (September 2008): 1986–2039.

10. Howard S. Bloom, Saskia Levy Thompson, and Rebecca Unterman, *Transforming the High School Experience: How New York City's New Small Schools Are Boosting Students Achievement and Graduation Rates* (New York: MDRC, 2010).

11. Janet C. Quint, Jannell K. Smith, Rebecca Unterman, and Alma E. Moedano, *New York City's Changing High School Landscape: High Schools and Their Characteristics, 2002–2008* (New York: MDRC, 2010).

12. Bloom, Thompson, and Unterman, *Transforming the High School Experience.*

13. W. David Sterns, *If Small Is Not Enough . . .? The Characteristics of Successful Small High Schools in Chicago* (Chicago: Consortium on Chicago School Research, 2008).

14. Dea R. Lillard and Philip P. DeCicca, "Higher Standards, More Dropouts? Evidence Within and Across Time," *Economics of Education Review* 20, no. 5 (2001): 459–473.

15. Debra Viadero, "Math Emerges as Big Hurdle for Teenagers," *Education Week,* March 23, 2005.

16. Lynn Olson, "Calls for Revamping High Schools Intensify," *Education Week,* January 26, 2005.

17. *College Completion: Additional Efforts Could Help Education with Its Completion Goals,* GAO-03-568 (Washington, DC: U.S. General Accounting Office, 2003).

18. Becky Bartindale, "Fewer Students Admitted to CSU," *San Jose Mercury News,* April 14, 2005, B1.

19. David J. Olender, "Budget Sparks Heated Debate," *Daily Aztec,* April 13, 2010, http://www.thedailyaztec.com/city/budget-sparks-heated-debate-1.2220471.

Chapter 11 .

1. Greg Brenneman, "Right Away and All at Once: How We Saved Continental," *Harvard Business Review* 76, no. 5 (1998): 162–172.

2. "Secretary of Education Arne Duncan: Remarks at the 2009 Governors Education Conference," June 14, 2009, http://www.hunt-institute.org/knowledge-library/articles/2009-6-29/video-sec-of-education-arne-duncan-at-the-2009-governors-education-symposium/.

3. Gilbert Cruz, "A Quick Fix for America's Worst Schools," *Time*, February 22, 2010, http://www.time.com/time/printout/0,8816,1963754,00.html.

4. Jennifer King Rice and Betty Malen, *School Reconstitution as an Education Reform Strategy: A Synopsis of the Evidence* (Washington, DC: National Education Association, 2010); see also David Bacon, "Workplace Reconstitution: The Clint Eastwood Solution for Low-Performing Schools," October 22, 1997, http://dbacon.igc.org/Work/02recnst.htm.

5. What Works Clearinghouse, *Turning Around Chronically Low-Performing Schools*, IES Practice Guide (Washington, DC: U.S. Department of Education, 2008).

6. Frederick M. Hess and Thomas Gift, "How to Turn Schools Around," *American School Board Journal* 195, no. 11 (2008), http://www.frederickhess.org/5133/how-to-turn-schools-around.

7. Betty Malen, Robert Croninger, Donna Muncey, and Donna Redmond-Jones, "Reconstituting Schools: 'Testing' the Theory of Action," *Educational Evaluation and Policy Analysis* 24, no. 2 (2002): 113–132.

8. Marisa de la Torre and Julia Gwynne, *When Schools Close: Effects on Displaced Students in Chicago Public Schools* (Chicago: Consortium on Chicago School Research, 2009), http://ccsr.uchicago.edu/content/publications.php?pub_id=136.

9. Brian Gill, Ron Zimmer, Jolley Christman, and Suzanne Blanc, *State Takeover, School Restructuring, Private Management, and Student Achievement in Philadelphia* (Santa Monica CA: RAND 2007), http://www.rand.org/pubs/monographs/MG533/.

10. Robert Manwaring, *Restructuring 'Restructuring': Improving Interventions for Low-Performing Schools and Districts* (Washington, DC: Education Sector, 2009), http://www.educationsector.org/research/research_show.htm?doc_id=1208019.

11. Brenda Neuman-Sheldon, *Making Mid-Course Corrections: School Restructuring in Maryland* (Washington DC: Center on Education Policy, 2007).

12. Caitlin Scott, *Improving Low-Performing schools: Lessons from Five Years of Studying School Restructuring under No Child Left Behind* (Washington, DC: Center on Education Policy, 2009).

13. Anthony S. Bryk et al., *Organizing Schools for Improvement: Lessons from Chicago* (Chicago: University of Chicago Press, 2010).

14. See Charles Payne, *So Much Reform, So Little Change: The Persistence of Failure in Urban Schools* (Cambridge, MA: Harvard Education Press, 2008), 189–190.

Chapter 12

1. Determining average class sizes is tricky because of the number of specialized (e.g., special education) teachers who may work with only a handful

of students. Typically, a school's average class size is calculated by dividing the number of students by the number of teachers, but most counts include specialized teachers, resulting in a number lower than the average number of students in regular classrooms.

2. Elizabeth Word et al., *Student/Teacher Achievement Ratio (STAR): Tennessee's K–3 Class Size Study,* Final Summary Report 1985–1990 (Nashville: Tennessee Department of Education, 1990).

3. Barbara A. Nyeet et al., *The Lasting Benefits Study: A Continuing Analysis of the Effect of Small Class Size in Kindergarten Through Third Grade on Student Achievement Test Scores in Subsequent Grade Levels,* Seventh Grade Technical Report (Nashville: Center of Excellence for Research in Basic Skills, 1994). An even more recent reanalysis of the STAR data found significant benefits from small classes (thirteen to seventeen students) in early grades (K–3) that lasted for students in grades 4–8, with low achievers showing strongest benefits in reading and science. See Spyros Konstantopoulos and Vicki Chung, "What Are the Long-Term Benefits of Small Classes on the Achievement Gap? Evidence from the Lasting Benefits Study," *American Journal of Education* 116, no. 1 (2009), http://www.journals.uchicago.edu/doi/abs/10.1086/605103.

4. Frederick Mosteller, "The Tennessee Study of Class Size in the Early Grades," *Critical Issues for Children and Youths* 5, no. 2 (1995).

5. George W. Bohrnstedt and Brian M. Stecher, eds., *What We Have Learned About Class Size Reduction in California* (Sacramento: California Department of Education, 2002).

6. Ivor Pritchard, *Reducing Class Size: What Do We Know?* U.S. Department of Education, March 1999, http://www.ed.gov/pubs/ReducingClass/title.html.

Chapter 13

1. William Schmidt et al., *Why Schools Matter: A Cross-National Comparison of Curriculum and Learning* (San Francisco: Jossey-Bass, 2001), 298–301, 308–309.

2. National Education Commission on Time and Learning, *Prisoners of Time,* May 1994, http://www.ed.gov/pubs/PrisonersOfTime/PoTSchool/intro.html; and Scot Lehigh, "The Case for Longer School Days," *Boston Globe,* January 19, 2005, http://www.boston.com/news/globe/editorial_opinion/oped/articles/2005/01/19/the_case_for_longer_school_days/. On how much time children between ages eight and eighteen watch media, including TV, computers, etc., see Kaiser Family Foundation, "Generation M2: Media in the Lives of 8–18 Year-Olds," http://www.kff.org/entmedia/mh012010pkg.cfm.

3. Center for American Progress, "Expanded Learning Time by the Numbers," Center for American Progress, April 22, 2010, http://www.americanprogress.org/issues/2010/04/elt_numbers.html.

4. Priscilla Pardini, "Extended School Days," *School Administrator,* August 2001, http://www.aasa.org/publications/sa/2001_08/pardini2.htm; National Association for Year-Round Education, "Statistical Summaries of Year-Round Education Programs, 2004–2005," http://www.nayre.org. Not all year-round

schools increase time in school. In many places where school construction has not kept pace with numbers of children attending school, particularly in urban low-income areas, school administrators switched to year-round education to accommodate larger numbers of students. By using the building all year and staggering school days and vacations for different groups of students, year-round schools solve the problem of overcrowded schools.

5. Dirk Johnson, "Many Schools Putting an End to Child's Play," *New York Times*, April 7, 1998. The Atlanta Public Schools have slowly reinstated recess since that superintendent exited. See Patti Ghezzi, "Atlanta Schools Bring Back Recess," *Atlanta Journal-Constitution*, September 21, 2006, A1.

6. Harris Cooper, "Summer Learning Loss: The Problem and Some Solutions," *ERIC Digest* (May 2003): EDO-PS-03-5.

7. Karl L. Alexander, Doris R. Entwisle, and Linda Steffel Olson, "Lasting Consequences of the Summer Learning Gap," *American Sociological Review* 72 (April 2007): 167–180.

8. Melissa Roderick, Mimi Engel, and Jenny Nagaoka, *Ending Social Promotion: Results from Summer Bridge* (Chicago: Consortium on Chicago School Research, 2003).

9. Geoffrey D. Borman and N. Maritza Dowling, "The Longitudinal Achievement Effects of Multi-Year Summer School: Evidence from the Teach Baltimore Randomized Field Trial," *Educational Evaluation and Policy Analysis* 28, no. 1 (2006): 25–48.

10. National Education Commission on Time and Learning, "Prisoners of Time," May 1994, http://www.ed.gov/pubs/PrisonersOfTime/PoTSchool/intro.html; Anthony Pellegrini and Catherine Bohn, "The Role of Recess in Children's Cognitive Performance and School Adjustment," *Education Researcher* 34 (January/February 2005): 13–19; An-Me Chung and Eugene Hillsman, "Evaluating After-School Programs," *School Administrator*, May 2005, http://www.aasa.org/publications/sa/2005_05/chung.htm (Retrieved May 20, 2005.); "Improving Student Achievement by Extending School: Is It Just a Matter of Time?" WestEd, 1998, http://www.wested.org/online_pubs/timeandlearning/TAL_PV.html.

Chapter 14

1. Ronald Edmonds, "Effective Schools for the Urban Poor," *Educational Leadership* 37, no. 1 (1979): 15–24.

2. Thomas J. Peters and Robert H. Waterman Jr., *In Search of Excellence: Lessons from America's Best-Run Companies* (New York: Harper & Row, 1982).

3. Kati Haycock and Karin Chenoweth, "Choosing to Make a Difference: How Schools and Districts Are Beating the Odds and Narrowing the Achievement Gap," *American School Board Journal* 192, no. 4 (2005): 23–31.

4. Michelle Clayman, "Excellence Revisited," *Financial Analysts Journal* 50, no. 3 (1994): 61–65.

5. See Richard Rothstein, *Class and Schools* (Washington, DC: Economic Policy Institute, 2004).

Chapter 15

1. Joe Smydo, "Performance Pay Slated for City Principals," *Pittsburgh Post-Gazette,* March 23, 2007, http://www.post-gazette.com/pg/07082/771912-298.stm; "$19.7 Million Awarded in Performance Bonuses to New York City Elementary and Middle School Educators," news release, NYC Department of Education, September 18, 2008, http://schools.nyc.gov/Offices/mediarelations/NewsandSpeeches/2008-2009/20080918_performance_bonuses.htm.

2. Elissa Gootman and Robert Gebeloff, "Principals Younger and Freer but Raise Doubts in Schools," *New York Times,* May 25, 2009, http://www.nytimes.com/2009/05/26/nyregion/26principals.html.

3. Larry Cuban, *The Managerial Imperative and the Practice of Leadership in Schools* (Albany: State University of New York Press, 1988), 53–54.

4. Philip Hallinger, "The Evolving Role of American Principals: From Managerial to Instructional to Transformation Leaders," *Journal of Educational Administration* 30, no. 3 (1992): 35–50; Linda Perlstein, *Tested* (New York: Henry Holt, 2007).

5. For an argument that principals should devote less time to supervision and more time to helping teams of teachers examine student work, see Richard DuFour and Robert J. Marzano, "High-Leverage Strategies for Principal Leadership," *Educational Leadership*, February 2009, 62–68.

6. New Leaders for New Schools, http://www.nlns.org/.

7. Jane L. David, "What Research Says About Classroom Walk-Throughs," *Educational Leadership,* December 2007/January 2008.

8. Ron Heck, "Principals' Instructional Leadership and School Performance: Implications for Policy Development," *Educational Evaluation and Policy Analysis* 14, no. 1 (1992): 21–34; Lynn Evans and Charles Teddlie, "Facilitating Change in Schools: Is There a One Best Style?" *School Effectiveness and School Improvement* 6, no. 1 (1995): 1–22; Kenneth Leithwood, "Understanding Successful Principal Leadership: Progress on a Broken Front," *Journal of Educational Administration* 43, no. 6 (2005): 619–629.

9. Robert Marzano, *What Works in Schools: Translating Research into Action* (Alexandria VA: ASCD, 2003).

10. Anthony S. Bryk, Penny Bender Sebring, Elaine Allensworth, Stuart Luppescu, and John Q. Easton, *Organizing Schools for Improvement: Lessons from Chicago* (Chicago: University of Chicago Press, 2010).

11. Of the many studies and books Cuban has examined, one in particular offers both a conceptual design and practical techniques to increase the leadership of principals in supervising and evaluating teachers, major functions of every school-site leader. See Kim Marshall, *Rethinking Teacher Supervision and Evaluation* (San Francisco: Jossey-Bass, 2009).

12. Brenda Turnbull et al., "Evaluation of the School Administration Manager Project," December 2009, http://www.ernweb.com/public/1175.cfm.

13. Half of Chicago principals are in the first four years of their job. Sara Ray Stoelinga, Holly Hart, and Dave Schalliol, *The Work of Chicago School Principals* (Chicago: Consortium on Chicago School Research, 2008).

Chapter 16

1. NAEP 2009 data cited in this chapter is found at http://nationsreportcard. gov/reading_2009/nat_g4.asp?subtab_id=Tab_3&tab_id=tab2#chart (fourth grade) and http://nationsreportcard.gov/reading_2009/nat_g8.asp?tab_id=tab2&subtab_id=Tab_3#chart (eighth grade).

2. National Institute of Child Health and Human Development, *Report of the National Reading Panel—Teaching Children to Read: An Evidence-Based Assessment of the Scientific Research Literature on Reading and Its Implications for Reading Instruction*, NIH Publication No. 00-4754 (Washington, DC: Government Printing Office, 2000), http://www.nationalreadingpanel.org/publications/subgroups.htm. See also Joann Yatvin, "Minority View," 2000, www.nichd.nih.gov/publications/nrp/minorityView.pdf. Other critiques include Siegfried Engelmann, "The Dalmation and Its Spots," *Education Week,* January 28, 2004; and Richard L. Allington, "Ideology Is Still Trumping Evidence," *Phi Delta Kappan,* February 2005, 462–468.

3. Catherine E. Snow, M. Susan Burns, and Peg Griffin, eds., *Preventing Reading Difficulties in Young Children* (Washington, DC: National Academy of Sciences, 1998).

4. Stanley Pogrow, "The Missing Element in Reducing the Learning Gap: Eliminating the 'Blank Stare,'" *Teachers College Record,* October 2004.

Chapter 17

1. In the fall of 2008, 37 percent of all freshman and 64 percent of African Americans admitted to the California State University system needed remediation in math. See http://www.asd.calstate.edu/remediation/08/Rem_Sys_fall2008.htm.

2. NAEP Long-Term Trends 2008, http://nationsreportcard.gov/ltt_2008/.

3. Debra Viadero, "Math Emerges as Big Hurdle for Teenagers," *Education Week,* March 23, 2005.

4. Robert Reys, "Reform Math Education," *Christian Science Monitor,* November 15, 2002, www.csmonitor.com/2002/1115/p09s01-coop.html.

5. Viadero, "Math Emerges," 16.

6. Students from higher-income families are almost twice as likely as lower-income students to take algebra in middle rather than high school. "Mathematics Equals Opportunity," October 1997, http://www.ed.gov/pubs/math/part2.html.

7. Sarah Theule Lubienski, Christopher Lubienski, and Corinna Crawford Crane, "Achievement Differences and School Type: The Role of School Climate, Teacher Certification, and Instruction," *American Journal of Education* 115 (November 2008): 97–138.

8. Thomas P. Carpenter, Elizabeth Fennema, Penelope L. Peterson, Chi-Pang Chiang, and Megan Loef, "Using Knowledge of Children's Mathematics Thinking in Classroom Teaching: An Experimental Study," *American Educational Research Journal* 26, no. 4 (1989): 499–531.

9. Heather C. Hill, Brian Rowan, and Deborah Loewenberg Ball, "Effects of Teachers' Mathematical Knowledge for Teaching on Student Achievement," *American Educational Research Journal* 42, no. 2 (2005): 371–406.

10. James Vaznis, "Aspiring Teachers Fall Short on Math," *Boston Globe*, May 19, 2009, http://www.boston.com/news/education/k_12/articles/2009/05/19/aspiring_teachers_fall_short_on_math/.

11. Patricia Clark Kenschaft, "Racial Equity Requires Teaching Elementary School Teachers More Mathematics," *Notices of the AMS* 52, no. 2 (2005): 208–212.

12. Ibid.

13. Larry Cuban, *How Teachers Taught: Constancy and Change in American Classrooms 1880–1990* (New York: Teachers College Press, 1993).

14. Sean Cavanagh, "Panel Calls for Systematic, Basic Approach to Math," *Education Week,* March 13, 2008, http://www.edweek.org/ew/articles/2008/03/19/28math_ep.h27.html.

15. Sharon Noguchi, 'Math Wars' over National Standards May Erupt Again in California," *San Jose Mercury News*, March 29, 2010, http://www.mercurynews.com/ci_14780292?IADID=Search-www.mercurynews.com-www.mercurynews.com.

Chapter 18

1. Jessica W. David and Kurt J. Bauman, *School Enrollment in the United States: 2006* (Washington, DC: U.S Census Bureau, 2008); Office of English Language Acquisition, *The Biennial Report to Congress on the Implementation of the Title III State Formula Grant Program, School Years 2004–06* (Washington, DC: U.S. Department of Education, 2008); U.S. Department of Education, *Building Partnerships to Help English Language Learners*, 2006, http://www2.ed.gov/print/nclb/methods/english/lepfactsheet.html. Because Hispanics are the largest group of immigrants, much of this chapter will focus on them.

2. National Center for Educational Statistics, *The Condition of Education 2003* (Washington, DC: U.S. Department of Education, 2003), 126.

3. Sam Anaya quoted in Mary Ann Zehr, "Oklahoma District Picks Path Less Followed for English-Learners," *Education Week*, May 4, 2005.

4. The German immigrant boy story is in Kenji Hakuta, *Mirror of Language* (New York: Basic Books, 1986), 207.

5. David Tyack, *The One Best System* (Cambridge, MA: Harvard University Press, 1974), 106–109.

6. Ibid.

7. Noel Epstein, *Language, Ethnicity, and the Schools* (Washington, DC: Institute for Educational Leadership, 1977), 1–3.

8. Michelle Adam, "The Changing Face of ELL Literacy Practices under No Child Left Behind," *ELL Outlook*, November/December 2004, http://www.coursecrafters.com/ELL-Outlook/2004/nov_dec/OutLook_NovDec.html.

9. NAEP, Reading, 2003, http://nces.ed.gov/nationsreportcard/reading/results 2003/scale-ethnic-compare.asp.

10. Interviewed by Jane David in 2003 as part of a study that promised anonymity to respondents.

11. James Crawford, "English Only vs. English Only: A Tale of Two Initiatives," http://ourworld.compuserve.com/homepages/JWCRAWFORD/203-227.htm.

12. Claude Goldenberg, "Teaching English Language Learners What the Research Does—and Does Not—Say," *American Education* 32, no. 2 (2008): 8–44, http://www.aft.org/pubs-reports/american_educator/issues/summer08/goldenberg.pdf.

13. Fred Genesee, Kathryn Lindholm-Leary, Bill Saunders, and Donna Christian, *Educating English Language Learners* (New York: Cambridge University Press, 2006).

14. Kenji Hakuta, Yuko Goto Butler, and Daria Witt, *How Long Does It Take English Learners to Attain Proficiency?* Policy Report 2000-1 (Berkeley: University of California Linguistic Minority Research Institute, 1999).

15. Vickie Lake and Eleni Pappamihiel, "Effective Practices and Principles to Support English Language Learners in Early Childhood Classrooms," *Childhood Education* 17, no. 2 (2003): 200–203; Wayne Thomas and Virginia Collier, *A National Study of School Effectiveness for Language Minority Students' Long-Term Academic Achievement* (Berkeley, CA: Center for Research on Education, Diversity, and Excellence, 2002); Kris Gutierrez et al., "Sounding American: The Consequences of New Reforms on English Language Learners," *Reading Research Quarterly* 37, no. 3 (2002): 328–345.

16. Goldenberg, "Teaching English Language Learners."

17. Guadalupe Valdes, *Con Respeto: Bridging the Distance Between Culturally Diverse Families and Schools* (New York: Teachers College Press, 1996).

Chapter 19

1. Jane L. David, Pamelia Coe, and Patricia J. Kannapel, *Content-Focused Professional Development in Kentucky: A Study of the Middle-School Summer Academies* (Lexington: Partnership for Kentucky Schools, 2003).

2. Sam Dillon, "'Soccer Mom' Education Chief Plays Hardball," *New York Times,* April 28, 2005.

3. Richard F. Elmore and Deanna Burney, "Investing in Teacher Learning: Staff Development and Instructional Improvement," in *Teaching as the Learning Profession: Handbook of Policy and Practice,* ed. Linda Darling-Hammond and Gary Sykes (San Francisco: Jossey-Bass, 1999).

4. Harold W. Stevenson and James W. Stigler, *The Learning Gap* (New York: Summit Books, 1992).

5. See the brief synthesis in G. Williamson McDiarmid, *Still Missing after All These Years: Understanding the Paucity of Subject-Matter Professional Development in Kentucky* (Lexington: Partnership for Kentucky Schools, 1999).

6. Mary Kennedy, *Form and Substance in In-Service Teacher Education* (Washington, DC: National Institute of Science Education, 1998).

7. Debra Viadero, "Coaching of Teachers Found to Boost Student Reading," *Education Week,* May 4, 2010, http://www.edweek.org/ew/articles/2010/05/04/31literacy.html?qs=literacy+collaborative.

8. Ronald Gallimore, Bradley A. Ermeling, William M. Saunders, and Claude Goldenberg, "Moving the Learning of Teaching Closer to Practice: Teacher Education Implications of School-Based Inquiry Teams," *Elementary School Journal* 109, no. 5 (2009): 537–553; Yvonne L. Goddard, Roger D. Goddard, and Megan Tschannen-Moran, "A Theoretical and Empirical Investigation of Teacher Collaboration for School Improvement and Student Achievement in Public Elementary Schools," *Teachers College Record* 109, no. 4 (2007): 877–896 ; Catherine C. Lewis, Rebecca Perry, Jacqueline Hurd, and Mary Pat O'Connell, "Lesson Study Comes of Age in North America," *Phi Delta Kappan* 88, no. 04 (2006): 273–281; Milbrey W. McLaughlin and Joan E. Talbert, *Developing Teacher Learning Communities in Schools: A Local Agenda to Improve Student Achievement* (New York: Teachers College Press, 2006).

9. Judith Warren Little, "Inside Teacher Community: Representations of Classroom Practice," *Teachers College Record* 105, no. 6 (2003): 913–945.

10. *A Nation at Risk: The Imperative for Educational Reform* (Washington, DC: National Commission on Excellence in Education, 1983), http://www2.ed.gov/pubs/NatAtRisk/recomm.html.

11. *Time for Learning,* Education Policy White Paper (Washington, DC: National Academy of Education, 2009).

Chapter 20

1. Andrew Zucker, *Transforming Schools with Technology* (Cambridge, MA: Harvard Education Press, 2008), 12–15.

2. Allan Collins and Richard Halverson, *Rethinking Education in the Age of Technology* (New York: Teachers College Press, 2009).

3. As of 2009, 84 percent of eight- to eighteen-year-olds have computers with Internet access at home; 59 percent have high-speed Internet access at home. Victoria J. Rideout, Ulla G. Foehr, and Donald F. Roberts, *Generation M^2 : Media in the Lives of 8- to 18-year-olds* (Menlo Park, CA : Kaiser Family Foundation, 2010).

4. Amy Hightower, "Tracking U.S. Trends," *Education Week*, March 26, 2009.

5. Ibid.

6. Ibid.

7. Andy Zucker and Sarah Hug, "Teaching and Learning Physics in a 1:1 Laptop School," *Journal of Science Education and Technology* 17, no. 6 (2008): 586–594.

8. Chris Kenning, "Student Faults Schools on Computer Use," *Courier-Journal,* July 12, 2005.

9. Holly M. Hart, Elaine Allensworth, Douglas L. Lauen, and Robert M. Gladden, *Educational Technology: Availability and Use in Chicago's Public Schools* (Chicago: Consortium on Chicago School Research, 2002).

10. Henry J. Becker, "Who's Wired and Who's Not: Children's Access to and Use of Computer Technology," *Future of Children* 10, no. 2 (2000): 44–75; Barbara Means, William R. Penuel, and Christine Padilla, *The Connected School: Technology and Learning in High School* (San Francisco: Jossey-Bass, 2001).

11. "Test Seeks to Measure Students Web IQ," *USA Today,* July 23, 2005.

12. Gordon MacInnes, *In Plain Sight: Simple, Difficult Lessons from New Jersey's Expensive Effort to Close the Achievement Gap* (New York: Century Foundation Press, 2009), 34–39.

Chapter 21

1. Suzanne Tacheny and Linda Plattner, "Giving 'Data' Its Own Assessment," *Education Week,* May 11, 2005.

2. See, for example, "U.S. Secretary of Education Margaret Spellings Delivers Remarks at the Aspen Institute's National Education Summit," September 15, 2008, http://www2.ed.gov/news/speeches/2008/09/09152008.html.

4. The $2 million annual Broad Prize is awarded to urban districts that demonstrate the greatest districtwide increases in achievement and evidence of closing the gap among poor and minority children. In a press release describing the former project director's study of award winners, the Broad Foundation identifies three main contributors to success: a rigorous curriculum aligned with standards, data-driven teaching and testing, and stable governance. See http://broadeducation.org/.

5. Daniel Koretz, *Measuring Up: What Educational Testing Really Tells Us* (Cambridge MA: Harvard University Press, 2008).

6. Meredith Kolodner and Rachel Monahan, "State Math Exam Scores Have Risen—but It's Because Tests Have Gotten Easier," *New York Daily News,* June 7, 2009.

7. Jeffrey C. Wayman, "Involving Teachers in Data-Driven Decision Making: Using Computer Data Systems to Support Teacher Inquiry and Reflection," *Journal of Education for Students Placed at Risk* 10, no. 3 (2005): 295–308.

8. Julie A. Marsh, John F. Pane, and Laura S. Hamilton, *Making Sense of Data-Driven Decision Making in Education: Evidence from Recent RAND Research* (Santa Monica CA: RAND, 2006).

9. Debra Ingram, Karen Seashore Louis, and Roger G. Schroeder, "Accountability Policies and Teacher Decision Making: Barriers to the Use of Data to Improve Practice," *Teachers College Record* 106, no. 6 (2004):1258–1287; Richard DuFour, Rebecca DuFour, Robert Eaker, and Gayle Karhanek, *Raising the Bar and Closing the Gap: Whatever It Takes* (Bloomington, IN: Solution Tree Press, 2010).

10. Paul Black et al., "Working Inside the Black Box: Assessment for Learning in the Classroom," *Phi Delta Kappan* 86, no. 1 (2004): 8–21.

Chapter 22

1. Emily Forrest Cataldi, Jennifer Laird, Angelina KewalRamani, and Chris Chapman, *High School Dropout and Completion Rates in the United States: 2007* (Washington, DC: National Center for Educational Statistics, 2009).

2. We use the phrase *multiple pathways* to mean varied high school curricula that offer college-level courses in technical education and career strands involving workplace internships and classroom projects. Sometimes this approach is called *linked learning*. In other parts of the country, however, multiple pathways refers to continuation schools, places where high school students who cannot adjust to regular programs finish their courses and get a diploma or general education degree (GED). See http://blogs.edweek.org/edweek/high-school-connections/2009/07/multiple_pathways_new_york_and.html?qs=multiple+pathways.

3. Examples drawn from Paul L . Heasley and William G. Van Der Sluys, "The State High Biodiesel Project," *Science Teacher* (April/May 2009): 26–31; TechEd Notes, September 15, 2009, http://technicaleducator.com/blog/?cat=16; and "The Core Connection: CTE and Academics: A Perfect Fit," Association for Career and Technical Education, 2003, http://www.thefreelibrary.com/The+core+connection:+CTE+and+academics:+a+perfect+fit.-a0107896835.

4. Kenneth Hoyt, "Career Education and Vocational Education: A Re-Examination," *Journal of Career Development* 6 (1980): 178–186.

5. *Edutopia* summary of research on project- and problem-based learning, November 1, 2001, http://www.edutopia.org/project-based-learning-research. Examples of current high schools that use project-based learning and internships are Providence, Rhode Island's, The Met (http://www.whatkidscando.org/archives/portfoliosmallschools/met/METintro.html) and a string of technology-based schools in Napa, California, and elsewhere called New Tech High Schools (http://www.newtechfoundation.org/) and Expeditionary Learning schools (http://www.elschools.org/) scattered across the nation.

6. Laura G. Knapp, Janice E. Kelly-Reid, and Scott A. Ginder, *Enrollment in Postsecondary Institutions, Fall 2007; Graduation Rates, 2001 and 2004 Cohorts; and Financial Statistics, Fiscal Year 2007* (Washington, DC: National Center for Education Statistics, 2009, http://nces.ed.gov/pubs2009/2009155.pdf.

7. Jill Casner-Lotto and Linda Barrington, *Are They Really Ready to Work? Employers' Perspective on the Basic Knowledge and Applied Skills of New Entrants to the 21st Century U.S. Workforce,* Conference Board, 2006, www.conference-board.org/pdf_free/BED-06-workforce.pdf.

8. James Kemple, *Career Academies: Long-Term Impacts on Labor Market Outcomes, Educational Attainment, and transitions to Adulthood* (New York: MDRC, 2008).

9. Jo Boaler, "Learning from Teaching: Exploring the Relationship Between Reform Curriculum and Equity," *Journal for Research in Mathematics Education* 33, no. 4 (2002): 239–258.

10. For a discussion of effective programs for retaining students and opportunities for those who have dropped out, see Paul Barton, *One-Third of a Nation: Rising Dropout Rates and Declining Opportunities* (Princeton, NJ: Educational Testing Service, 2005).

Chapter 23

1. Elizabeth Rich, "A Custom Fit," *Teacher Magazine*, April 12, 2010, 26.
2. Robert Wedl, "Response to Intervention: An Alternative to Traditional Eligibility Criteria for Students with Disabilities," *Education Evolving*, July 2005; Laura Justice, "Evidence-Based Practice, Response to Intervention, and the Prevention of Reading Difficulties," *Language, Speech, and Hearing Services in Schools* 37 (2006): 284–297; Kate Rix, "Your Guide to RTI: The Latest in Response to Intervention (RTI)," http://www2.scholastic.com/browse/article.jsp?id=3749549.
3. Anthony Rebora, "Responding to RTI," *Education Week*, April 12, 2010, 20.
4. For special education statistics, see *Digest of Educational Statistics: Table 50*, 2008, http://nces.ed.gov/programs/digest/d08/tables/dt08_050.asp.
5. For expenditures on special education, see Thomas Parrish, Jenifer Harr, Jean Wolman, Jennifer Anthony, Amy Merickel, and Phil Esra, *State Special Education Finance Systems, 1999–2000: Part II, Special Education Revenues and Expenditures* (Palo Alto, CA: American Institutes of Research, 2004), 28.
6. Lisa Fine, "Get to Know Alexa Posny, Head of OSERS, Part 2," *Education Week*, January 22, 2010, http://blogs.edweek.org/edweek/speced/2010/01/get_to_know_alexa_posny_head_o_1.html?qs=Get_to_Know_Alexa_Posny.
7. Rich, "A Custom Fit," 26.
8. Donald MacMillan and Gary Siperstein, "Learning Disabilities as Operationally Defined by Schools," paper presented at Learning Disabilities Summit, Washington, DC, August 27–28, 2001. Statistics for LD students are under Indicator 31 in *The Condition of Education 2007* (Washington, DC: National Center for Education Statistics, 2007), 68.
9. Douglas Fuchs and Lynn Fuchs, "Introduction to Response to Intervention: What, Why, and How Valid Is It?" *Reading Research Quarterly* 41, no. 1 (2006): 93–99; quote cited in MacMillan and Siperstein, "Learning Disabilities," 1.
10. Fuchs and Fuchs, "Introduction to Response to Intervention"; and for funding, see Anna Munson, "Federal Funding to Support Response to Intervention," RTI Action Network (National Center for Learning Disabilities), http://www.rtinetwork.org/GetStarted/Develop/ar/Federal-Funding-to-Support-Response-to-Intervention.
11. Christina Samuels, "'Response to Intervention' Sparks Interest, Questions," *Education Week*, January 18, 2008, http://www.edweek.org/ew/articles/2008/01/23/20rtireact.h27.html?tmp=1415039948.
12. Janette Klingner and Patricia Edwards, "Cultural Considerations with Response to Intervention Models," *Reading Research Quarterly* 41, no. 1 (2006): 108–117.

13. Ibid.; Fuchs and Fuchs, "Introduction to Response to Intervention."
14. Fuchs and Fuchs, "Introduction to Response to Intervention"; Samuels, "'Response to Intervention' Sparks Interest"; Amanda Vanderheyden, "RTI and Math Instruction," RTI Action Network (National Center for Learning Disabilities), http://www.rtinetwork.org/Learn/Why/ar/RTIandMath/1.
15. Charles Hughes and Douglas D. Dexter, "Field Studies of RTI Programs," Penn State University, http://www.rtinetwork.org/Learn/Research/ar/Field-Studies.
16. Rich, "A Custom Fit," 26; Klingner and Edwards, "Cultural Considerations," 108–117.

Chapter 23

1. Richard Elmore quoted in Marjorie Coeyman, "Just When You Thought You Knew the Rules," *Christian Science Monitor,* July 9, 2002, http://www.csmonitor.com/2002/0709/p11s01-lepr.html.
2. Job Outlook 2005, http://www.naceweb.org/press/display.asp?year=2005&prid=207.
3. Richard B. Anderson, Robert G. St. Pierre, Elizabeth C. Proper, and Linda B. Stebbins, "Pardon Us, but What Was the Question Again? A Response to the Critique of the Follow Through Evaluation," *Harvard Educational Review* 48, no. 2 (1978): 161–170.
4. Milbrey W. McLaughlin, "The Rand Change Agent Study Revisited: Macro Perspectives and Micro Realities," *Educational Researcher*, December 1990, 11–16.
5. See, for example, Larry Cuban, *How Teachers Taught* (New York: Teachers College Press, 1993); and Cynthia Coburn, "Collective Sensemaking About Reading: How Teachers Mediate Reading Policy in Their Professional Communities," *Educational Evaluation and Policy Analysis* 23, no. 2 (2001): 145–170.
6. Education Testing Service, "Public Opinion Poll," June 22, 2005, http://www.cpwire.com/archive/2005/6/22/1856.asp.
7. Patrick M. Shields, Camille E. Esch, Daniel C. Humphrey, Marjorie E. Wechsler, Christopher M. Chang-Ross, Alix H. Gallagher, Roneeta Guha, Juliet D. Tiffany-Morale, and Katrina R. Woodworth, *The Status of the Teaching Profession* (Santa Cruz, CA: Center for the Future of Teaching and Learning, 2003).
8. See, for example, a series of papers presented at the symposium entitled "Social Costs of Inadequate Education," Teachers College, Columbia University, October 2005, http://www.tc.columbia.edu/centers/EquitySymposium/symposium/resource.asp.

About the Authors

Jane L. David received a doctorate in education and social policy from Harvard University in 1974 after teaching high school mathematics in Washington, D.C. Since then, her career in research and evaluation has focused on the connections between education policy and how schools and districts improve, particularly those serving children at risk of failure. She directs the Bay Area Research Group, a small consulting firm whose clients range from think tanks and government agencies to foundations, districts, and nonprofit organizations. She also conducts strategic reviews for nonprofit organizations and foundations. David has authored more than a hundred reports, book chapters, articles, and commissioned papers and writes a bimonthly research column for *Educational Leadership*.

Larry Cuban is Professor Emeritus of Education at Stanford University. He has taught courses in the methods of teaching social studies, the history of school reform, the history of curriculum and instruction, and leadership. He has been faculty sponsor of the Stanford/Schools Collaborative and Stanford's Teacher Education Program.

Trained as a historian, Cuban received a BA from the University of Pittsburgh in 1955 and an MA from Cleveland's Western Reserve University in 1958. He subsequently taught high school social studies in urban schools for fourteen years and directed a teacher education program that prepared returning Peace Corps volunteers to teach in inner-city schools. On completing his PhD work at Stanford University in 1974, he assumed the superintendency of the Arlington (Virginia) Public Schools, a position he held until returning to Stanford in 1981.

Since 1988, he has taught three times in local high schools' semester-long courses in U.S. history and economics. Between 1981 and 2001, students in the School of Education selected Cuban seven times for an excellence in teaching award.

Cuban's major research interests focus on the history of curriculum and instruction, educational leadership, and school reform and the uses of technology in classrooms. His most recent books are *As Good as It Gets: What School Reform Brought to Austin* (2010) and *Hugging the Middle: How Teachers Teach in an Era of Testing and Accountability* (2009).

Index